Lives after Vietnam

Lives after Vietnam

The Personal Impact of Military Service

Josefina J. Card
American Institutes for Research
in the Behavioral Sciences

LexingtonBooks
D.C. Heath and Company
Lexington, Massachusetts
Toronto

Library of Congress Cataloging in Publication Data

Card, Josefina J.
    Lives after Vietnam.

    Bibliography: p.
    Includes index.
    1. Veterans—United States. 2. Vietnamese Conflict, 1961–1975.
I. Title.
UB357.C3   1983   355.1'15'0973   82-49119
ISBN 0–669–06420–3

Copyright © 1983 by D.C. Heath and Company

Published simultaneously in Canada

Printed in the United States of America

International Standard Book Number: 0–669–06420–3

Library of Congress Catalog Card Number: 82-49119

To Stu, Gwyneth, and Tiffany

Contents

Figures

Tables

Preface

This book is about military service in the Vietnam era. It is based on the experiences of a group of men, now in their mid-thirties, who were in the ninth grade in 1960 and thus, in the main, completed high school in 1963, the year before the official start of the Vietnam era. During the 1960s, one-half of these men served in the military; one-fifth were sent to the Vietnam war zone. In what ways were the men who served in the military different from their former classmates who never served? Among those who served, in what ways were the men assigned to Vietnam different from those assigned to more-peaceful areas of the world? How did the military and combat experiences of veterans affect their future schooling and work attainment, their physical and psychological health, their marriages and families, and their subsequent enjoyment of life? Were the effects of military service greater for those who fought in Vietnam than for those who were assigned to other areas of the world where there was no fighting? These are the main questions answered by the book.

The study focuses on three groups of men:

Group 1, the Vietnam veterans: A sample of approximately 500 men who served in the Vietnam war zone during the 1960s,

Group 2, the non-Vietnam veterans: Approximately 500 classmates who served in the military during the same period but were never assigned to Vietnam,

Group 3, the nonveterans: Approximately 500 classmates who never served in the military.

All 1,500 men had first been studied as ninth graders (in 1960) and then again eleven years after high school, in 1974, as part of a larger effort known as Project TALENT, a study of the career potential and achievements of Americans who were in high school in 1960. In early 1981, eighteen years after the date of their expected high-school graduation, when the men were around thirty-six years old, we surveyed them again for purposes of the present study.

In the initial 1960 survey, comprehensive information was obtained on the men's academic abilities, their vocational and avocational interests, their personalities, their home life, and their plans regarding further schooling, work, and military service. For purposes of the present study, this vast amount of information was used to select comparison groups (groups 2 and 3) that, with the help of appropriate case weights, could be matched with the main group of interest (group 1) in terms of socioeconomic and family background, as well as academic abilities, interests, and career plans. We wanted to be able to isolate which differences at midlife were attributable to the veterans' service and combat experiences, as opposed to preexisting differences between those who served and those who did not. Working with samples of comparable socio-demographic background and academic abilities enabled us to accomplish this work with more precision than is usually found in other studies of veterans and their peers.

We also wanted to be able to study the early predictors of military service in the Vietnam era: who in the class served in this war and who did not. To answer questions relative to this issue, we developed a different set of case weights that made the 1,500 Vietnam veterans, non-Vietnam veterans, and nonveterans in our sample representative of all Vietnam veterans, non-Vietnam veterans, and nonveterans in the ninth-grade class of 1960.

Our findings are generalizable to a whole grade group or cohort of men (the 1.1 million men who were in the ninth grade in 1960 and who were still alive twenty-one years later, at age thirty-six). This does not mean that they are not applicable to other surviving Vietnam-era soldiers as well. It means only that soldiers from other classes were not represented in our study. In the light of the changing nature of the Vietnam conflict through the war years, we need to be conservative and not assume, without corroborating evidence, that our results apply to them too.

A single-cohort or single-group study such as ours has this limitation. There is, however, an offsetting advantage: we can be more precise about our findings because all of the men in our study were of approximately the same age, and all of them grew up in the same historical, economic, social, and political era. Everyday observation tells us that men's income tends to rise with age and experience; unless great care is taken in analysis and interpretation, comparing raw income figures from men of different ages can be misleading. The problem persists if we compare the incomes of men of different ages at a given point in their life course (say, age thirty); different economic conditions at the time the various age cohorts turned thirty could also lead to misleading conclusions. Studying a single cohort allows us to document with maximum precision how a historical event such as the Vietnam war affected individual lives.

The men comprise a good cohort to study, given our goal of documenting the antecedents and personal consequences of Vietnam-era service. They are very close to (within a year of) the average age of the Vietnam-era soldier; they graduated from high school in 1963, a couple of years before the draft gained momentum and they contain large subgroups of both enlisted and drafted soldiers. A large proportion of the men were in Vietnam during the height of the fighting (the 1968 Tet offensive); thus a wide range of combat experiences—from none to heavy—is represented.

In the light of widespread interest in the topic covered by this study, the book has been directed to a wide audience. We believed it was important that the design of the study, the procedures used, the statistical analyses conducted, and the results be presented in a language and style understandable to the general college-educated reader. We also considered it equally important that social scientists be provided with sufficient information to evaluate the scientific merit of the work and to compare results from related investigations against findings obtained in the present one. Throughout the book, the organization of material, the layout of tables and figures, and the choice of words represent a compromise aimed at meeting the needs and interests of nonspecialists as well as specialists. We hope the result is a book that will be useful to soldiers and prospective soldiers; to vocational counselors in high schools and colleges; to military recruiters; to legislators, policymakers, and their staffs; to graduate and undergraduate students of the behavioral sciences; and to the growing numbers of sociologists and psychologists interested in military-personnel research, career-development research, and life-span development research.

Chapter 1 provides the historical background for the study and describes the research methods used. Chapter 2 details the antecedents of Vietnam-era service by providing comprehensive profiles of the three groups of interest and describing who in the ninth-grade class of 1960 served in the Vietnam era and who in the same class did not. Chapters 3 through 6 give the consequences of military service and of combat for veterans' subsequent educational attainment, occupational attainment, physical, social, and psychological health, and family and personal life. Both short-term consequences, measured at age twenty-nine, as well as longer-term consequences, measured at age thirty-six, are described. In addition, whenever possible, the moving picture through time—portraying the men's progress on these life dimensions from high school to the present—is presented. We have tried to show not only what the men were like at ages fifteen, twenty-nine, and thirty-six but also—with the help of their retrospective reconstructions of the interim periods—by what route and how rapidly they got there. This is important not only because the moving picture is inherently more complete than a couple of still pictures but also because still snapshots occasionally lead to misleading conclusions as a result of atypical economic and political conditions occurring in particular years. Finally, whenever possible, we have presented the different effects of military service for men from different family, socioeconomic, and ability backgrounds; for men who entered the service under varying degrees of coercion; for men who conducted themselves in different ways while in the service; and for men who experienced varying intensities of combat. The goal has been to document not just whether military service is generally helpful or harmful but also for whom, and under what circumstances. The result, we hope, is an accurate and comprehensive picture of the antecedents and consequences of military service in the Vietnam era for the 1.1 million men who were in the ninth grade in 1960.

Chapter 7 summarizes these antecedents and consequences and discusses implications of our findings for future groups of young men who may be faced with decisions similar to those encountered by the high-school class of 1963.

Acknowledgments

The research reported in this book was supported by grant MH34643 from the National Institute of Mental Health. The contributions of project staff are gratefully acknowledged. William S. Farrell conducted a literature review at the beginning of the project. He and Frances Stancavage then drafted the survey instrument with consulting assistance from a National Advisory Panel consisting of Warren B. Miller, a research psychiatrist at the American Institutes for Research (AIR); Gerald Moylan, a retired Marine Corps gunnery sergeant and veteran of both the Korean and Vietnam wars; and Vincent Zarcone, a professor of clinical psychiatry and behavioral sciences at the Palo Alto Veterans Administration. Farrell, Sharon McVicker, Kathleen Carrell, and James Folk located target respondents and solicited their cooperation. The fact that a location-cooperation rate of over 80 percent was achieved with a study population first studied more than twenty years ago is a tribute to their dedication and effectiveness. Farrell, McVicker, and Mary Hurst, in addition, coded the 1,500 questionnaires as they came in with impressive speed and accuracy. Virginia David typed the data tables and drafted the figures. Joe Leitner prepared camera-ready copy of the figures. Patricia Spurr, Richard Carter, and William Farrell provided editorial suggestions for improving the text. Jean Reynolds saw the manuscript through several drafts at the AIR word-processing center.

Special thanks are due to Lauress L. Wise, director of Project TALENT, who designed the study samples and devised the case weights used in all analyses. Winnie Young, Elizabeth DeVincenzi, and Standish Sibley constructed the data files and conducted the analyses with the help of the SPSS and SAS statistical packages. An internal panel of AIR scientists—Robert Krug, chief scientist; Sandra Wilson, director of the Institute for Health Care Research; Warren Miller; Lauress Wise; and Lauri Steel, associate director of Project TALENT—along with three anonymous outside reviewers, reviewed the manuscript for scientific merit and provided many helpful suggestions for improvement.

The design and execution of the present study benefited from ideas generated during the 1980 Summer Institute on Life-Span Human Development sponsored by the Center for Advanced Study in the Behavioral Sciences and the Social Science Research Committee on Life Course Perspectives on Middle Age. David Featherman; Paul Baltes; Orville G. Brim, Jr.; Matilda Riley; Glen Elder; and many others showed the importance of separating the effects of age, cohort, and period in our research.

Bob Krug and Bert Brim have been steady sources of personal and professional encouragement.

Finally, the study could not have been conducted without the cooperation of the 1,500 respondents who gave so generously of their time to the present study.

I acknowledge, with great thanks, the contributions of all these people.

1

Background and Methods

The American Veteran

Between one-quarter and four-fifths of men born in each year of this century through 1950 have served on active duty in the U.S. armed forces. The military-service demands on successive age groups or cohorts of men have been an important aspect of their history, causing generational differences in the experience of the passage from adolescence to adulthood. In this book, we examine the aftermath of military service for one group of men subjected to relatively extensive military-service demands: those who were in the ninth grade in 1960. Half of the men in this class enlisted or were drafted into service in the early years of the Vietnam era. We look at how Vietnam-era service affected the progress of their life course as they grew up from students and soldiers of the 1960s to workers and citizens of the 1980s.

Hogan (1981) describes how military service has had different educational and occupational consequences for different generations. For men born before 1939 (the World War I, World War II, and Korean war generations), military service was associated with an older age at completion of schooling, presumably because military service interrupted the normal course of education. Veterans often returned to school after military service; however, by this time, their age-mates had finished school and were in the labor force. This trend was reversed for men born after 1946 (the Vietnam generation), with civilians completing school, on average, at a later age than their veteran peers, possibly because Selective Service policies provided military-service deferments to men enrolled in college. Veterans' education, however, continued to be interrupted to a much greater extent than the education of their civilian peers.

Hand in hand with these educational consequences of military service has been the disruption of what sociologists call the orderly passage to adulthood: first complete school, then get a job, and finally get married. Because of veterans' relatively advanced age at service exit, they have often married prior to completing school or beginning work. Such a pattern has been associated with lower earnings at midlife among civilians. Veterans who have gone to college after their military stint, however, have not been similarly handicapped. Indeed, for the veterans of World War I, World War II, and the Korean war, military service in combination with a postmilitary college education was advantageous in terms of early career earnings, although this initial advantage eventually disappeared by mid-adulthood. While veterans of the Vietnam war who completed their college

1

education under the GI bill have not been similarly advantaged in the early years of reentry into the civilian labor force (possibly because of the national trauma associated with this latest conflict and consequent homecoming problems suffered by the veterans), they have not been unduly handicapped either (Hogan 1981). Possession of a college degree has continued to be a good investment for veterans.

Little is known about the long-term psychological and social readjustment of veterans from World War I, World War II, and the Korean war. After World War I, veterans were largely ignored. Partially as a result, they became politicized, banding together into veteran groups such as the Veterans of Foreign Wars and the American Legion. They demanded and got some benefits, including disability and pension payments. Their primary contribution may have been raising the consciousness of government and the public; both were much better prepared to deal with veterans of World War II.

World War II was unique for several reasons: it was the largest war the United States has ever fought, it was the most popular war in terms of homefront support, and it was the only war in which U.S. territory was actually attacked. Soldiers were highly studied during the war and its immediate aftermath (as for example, in the classic studies on *The American Soldier* by Stouffer and his colleagues and on soldier ineffectiveness by Ginzburg and his colleagues) but little studied after their return to civilian life after the war. A series of fortuitous circumstances made the largest demobilization in history, involving around 10 million men, go fairly smoothly. The economy was strong; the public welcomed veterans back; the Serviceman's Readjustment Act (GI Bill of Rights, 1944) allowed huge numbers of veterans to go to school, thus softening their impact on the labor market and increasing their marketable skills; finally, legislation regarding employment preferences for veterans was enacted. Although there was little scientific study of veterans' social and psychological adjustment as citizens, available evidence suggests that there were no major problems.

Soldiers in the Korea conflict were less studied than soldiers from World War II. This war was similar in magnitude to the war in Vietnam with respect to numbers of servicemen killed and wounded, but it did not last as long. It was neither a particularly popular nor unpopular war. GI benefits were expanded somewhat, and veterans, again because of a fairly strong economy, appeared to have little trouble reintegrating themselves into society.

Vietnam was a unique war in many respects. It was the longest conflict this country has ever been engaged in, yet war was never officially declared. It was a guerrilla war: there were no front lines, no easy demarcation of friend and foe. The war was fought with the assistance of high technology: combat units were armed with the latest, most-modern weapons; advances in medical technology kept a relatively high proportion of disabled veterans alive. Service in Vietnam was for twelve months instead of the duration of the war, leading to lower cohesion within combat units and to combat-withdrawal behavior as the contractual tour of duty reached its end. It was a war fought by the young: the average age of the Vietnam-era soldier was twenty-three; that of the World War II soldier was twenty-seven. Advances in the nation's educational attainments were in evidence. On separation from the military, 80 percent of Vietnam-era veterans had completed high school, as opposed to forty-five percent of World War II veterans. The Vietnam war was fought by men in the middle range of ability and socioeconomic status. The truly disadvantaged could not pass the mental and physical preinduction examinations; the truly advantaged managed to avoid service with the help of educational deferments. Drugs and alcohol were readily available in Vietnam, and substance abuse marked many servicemen's military stints. Perhaps most difficult of all from the point of view of combatants, the Vietnam war was the country's least-popular war and one that the United States failed to win. Home was not a cozy place to return to after the tour of duty, especially for those who returned in the latter years of the conflict. The late 1960s and early 1970s were marked by economic recession, high unemployment, and snowballing antiwar protests. Vietnam was the only war where veterans organized protest movements against U.S. involvement in the fighting. Perhaps for all these reasons, the social and psychological consequences of Vietnam-era service for the individuals involved in the conflict have been much more studied than those for any previous war in U.S. history. Findings from these various investigations will be described in the chapters to come, and the present study's findings will be related to what is known, controversial, or unknown.

The Population of Interest

The study reported here builds on the extensive samples and data in Project TALENT, a large-scale research project begun at the American Institutes for Research in 1960. In the spring of that year, 375,000 Americans, representative of the 8 million students then in high school (grades 9 to 12), spent two days filling out questionnaires and taking a battery of tests. These efforts provided extensive information on the family background, aptitudes, abilities, interests, personalities, educational experiences, activities, and plans of a whole generation of Americans. Several longitudinal follow-ups of TALENT participants have since been conducted (one, five, and eleven years after participants' expected high-school graduation date) in order to identify factors that have helped or hindered America's youth in their transition to adulthood and in order to provide suggestions to educators and policymakers on how the nation's human resources could be utilized better.

In 1979 the National Institute of Mental Health issued a Request for Proposals calling for the submission of research proposals to document the consequences of military service in the Vietnam era. A proposal to resurvey 1,500 carefully chosen TALENT participants for this purpose was submitted and approved. The present study was born.

Several unique benefits could be gained by an in-depth study of the lives of veterans and nonveterans in Project TALENT. First, men in the TALENT population were nineteen to twenty-two years old when the Vietnam era began in

1964. Thus they were subject to the draft that began in earnest the following year. Second, statistical weighting procedures had previously been developed by TALENT staff, allowing specially chosen subsamples such as those employed in the present study to be representative of the entire 1960 high-school population from which they were drawn (Wise 1977; Abeles and Wise 1979–1980). Third, the wealth of data already existing on TALENT participants would allow controls to be introduced that would not otherwise be possible in a nationwide survey. The study would have the power to attribute differences between veterans and nonveterans to the military experience of the veterans, to pre-existing differences between those who served and those who did not, or to both sources. Finally, the longitudinal nature of the TALENT data base would allow documentation of the antecedents of Vietnam-era service, as well as its short-term and long-term consequences. We found considerable disagreement in the literature about whether the job-related and psychological problems of veterans were long lasting or evanescent. We believed that the existence in TALENT of data collected at different times could shed light on some aspects of this controversy.

An early decision was made to limit the sample for the present study to male TALENT participants who were in the ninth grade in 1960 (the class of 1963) and who responded to the TALENT eleven-year post–high school follow-up survey conducted in 1974. Several considerations guided this choice of study respondents:

1. The study was limited to males because few women saw action in the Vietnam conflict.

2. The study was limited to those who were in the ninth grade in 1960 for two reasons. Of the four grade levels (nine to twelve) surveyed in 1960, ninth graders were the group most likely to have been subject to the draft and to have served in Vietnam. Members of the ninth-grade cohort were closest to the average Vietnam veteran with respect to age, being only a half-year older than the average Vietnam-era soldier. (In contrast, members of the tenth-, eleventh-, and twelfth-grade cohorts were 1.5 to 3.5 years older than the average Vietnam-era soldier.) Second, any TALENT sample, because it involves people who were in high school in 1960, potentially underrepresents individuals on the lowest extremes of mental and physical abilities: those who never reached high school are excluded from the TALENT populations. Ninth graders are the least biased in this sense, however, since those in this grade cohort who dropped out in grades 10, 11, or 12 are included. It is important to note that military preinduction examinations also eliminate individuals who do not meet minimum physical- and mental-ability standards. Thus the upward bias of the TALENT population is actually in line with the upward bias of military selection.

3. Finally, the study was limited to respondents to the TALENT 1974 follow-up survey to help ensure the high participation rate crucial to the validity

of a national survey such as this one. All of these sample members had participated in a similar survey in 1974. Because of the way they were selected and weighted for that prior survey, they continued to be representative of the ninth-grade class of 1960.[1]

The Class of 1963 Goes to War

Most of the men in our study population were born in 1945 or 1946. They were among the first of the post–World War II baby-boom generation, born as this country basked in that victory. They attended high school in the years between Sputnik and the flower children, when America's emphasis on educational attainment in general—and on scientific and technological training in particular—was at an all-time high. They were among the first to participate in the new math and accelerated science programs, as well as in many other experimental educational programs. Perhaps because of this emphasis on cognitive achievement, average verbal and mathematics scores on the Scholastic Aptitude Test reached a peak in 1963, the year our study subjects were seniors in high school, a peak that has not been matched since. In June 1963, they graduated from high school. In the same month, the first of seven Buddhist monks to commit suicide by fire in protest against the repression of the Diem regime died in Saigon. Five months later, a military coup overthrew Diem, killing him and his brother Ngo Dinh Nhu. General Duong Van Minh, head of the Revolutionary Military Committee, took over leadership of South Vietnam.

One year after our men's graduation from high school, North Vietnamese torpedo boats attacked the American destroyers U.S.S. *Maddox* and U.S.S. *C. Turner Joy*. American Seventh Fleet carrier aircraft retaliated by attacking the bases used by the torpedo boats and other military targets in North Vietnam. The U.S. Congress adopted the Tonkin Gulf Resolution endorsing whatever measures the president considered necessary to repel attacks on American forces and to prevent further aggression. The total U.S. troop strength in South Vietnam was 23,000.

In 1965, two years after our men's graduation from high school, the Vietcong attacked the U.S. base at Pleiku, South Vietnam. U.S. Air Force and South Vietnamese planes retaliated by attacking military targets in North Vietnam. The first U.S. Marine infantry battalion arrived at Da Nang, South Vietnam. The U.S. Army's 173d Airborne Brigade landed in South Vietnam. The draft of young American men started to gain momentum. Antiwar demonstrations became widespread throughout the United States. The total U.S. troop strength in South Vietnam was 181,000. Men from the high-school class of 1963 began enlisting or being drafted in earnest. They were twenty years old.

The war progressed in 1966 and 1967. At the end of these years, U.S. troop strength in South Vietnam stood at 385,000 and 486,000, respectively. In early 1968, the fighting reached its peak. In January 1968, the North Vietnamese Tet offensive erupted throughout South Vietnam, lasting until late February. On March 16, the My Lai massacre took place. On March 31, President Johnson announced that he would not seek reelection. Two months later, Johnson accepted a North Vietnamese offer to conduct preliminary peace discussions in Paris. In November 1968, President Richard Nixon was elected, promising a gradual troop withdrawal from Vietnam. U.S. troop strength at the end of 1968 stood at an all-time high: 536,100.

The U.S. presence declined in the following years, in keeping with Nixon's policy of Vietnamizing the war, falling to 474,000 at the end of 1969 and to 335,800 at the end of 1970. These years marked the beginning of our men's return to the United States. They returned to witness large-scale protests against the war they had just participated in. In May 1970, as antiwar demonstrations continued on a number of U.S. college campuses, four Kent State University students were fatally shot by members of the Ohio National Guard, triggering even more protests at some 400 colleges across the country. In April 1971, a half-million antiwar protesters converged on Washington D.C.; at least 150,000 more took part in similar demonstrations in San Francisco. By the end of 1972, only 27,000 American troops were left in South Vietnam.

Early the following year, Henry Kissinger of the United States and Le Duc Tho of North Vietnam initialed an agreement ending the war and providing for the release of prisoners of war. By the end of March 1973, the last American troops had left South Vietnam. In April, the last Americans held prisoner in North Vietnam arrived at Clark Air Base in the Philippines. The draft had ceased; most soldiers from the class of 1963 had made the transition to civilian life in the United States. The war between North and South Vietnamese forces continued in 1974 and 1975 until April 30, 1975, when President Duong Van Minh of South Vietnam announced his country's unconditional surrender.[2]

The following week, on May 7, 1975, President Gerald R. Ford proclaimed an end to the Vietnam era. The proclamation (see figure 1–1) fixed the official period of era service as beginning on August 5, 1964, and ending on May 7, 1975. It was a period in American history that lasted ten years, nine months, and two days.

Critique of Existing Studies of the Vietnam-Era Soldier

Many contradictions exist in the literature concerning the size and permanence of effects of both Vietnam-era military service in general and combat in particular. The inconsistencies generally have been caused by methodological limitations inherent in the studies. Most of them have been plagued by one or more limitations.

Some studies have studied veterans or combat veterans, without including a control group of nonveterans. Are the problems documented by these studies

---

BY THE PRESIDENT OF THE UNITED STATES OF AMERICA

A PROCLAMATION

The Congress has provided that entitlement to certain veterans benefits be limited to persons serving in the Armed Forces during the period, beginning August 5, 1964, referred to as the Vietnam era. The President is authorized to determine the last day on which a person must have entered the active military, naval, or air service of the United States in order for such service to qualify as service during that period.

The signing of the cease-fire agreements and implementing protocols on January 27, 1973, between the United States of America and the Republic of Vietnam, on the one hand, and the Democratic Republic of Vietnam and the Provisional Revolutionary Government of the Republic of South Vietnam on the other hand, has terminated active participation by the Armed Forces of the United States in the Vietnam conflict.

NOW, THEREFORE, I, GERALD R. FORD, President of the United States of America, by virtue of the authority vested in me by Section 101(29) of Title 38 of the United States Code, do hereby proclaim, for the purposes of said Section 101(29), that May 7, 1975, is designated as the last day of the "Vietnam era."

IN WITNESS WHEREOF, I have hereunto set my hand this seventh day of May in the Year of our Lord nineteen hundred seventy-five, and of the Independence of the United States of America the one hundred ninety-ninth.

GERALD R. FORD

Figure 1-1. Presidential Proclamation Ending the Vietnam Era

attributable to the military experience of the men? Without a control group of men who did not undergo the military experience, one cannot say.

Other studies have included a control group of nonveterans, but the control group has not been matched with the veteran group in terms of preservice characteristics. Are the differences between unmatched groups of veterans and nonveterans attributable to the military experience of the veterans or to the fact that the groups were different to begin with (for example, in terms of academic ability or socioeconomic status)? Unless one takes into account the preservice characteristics of the groups, one cannot tell.

Even when information on preservice characteristics has been included, it has usually been obtained retrospectively. Subjects have been asked to recall what their lives were like as children, adolescents, and young adults. While certain information such as family demographics (such as father's occupation) and important transition dates (such as year of high-school graduation or year of first marriage) can usually be remembered and reported accurately, other information, such as one's early educational and career plans, or one's past attitudes, cannot always be remembered accurately. Recollections are often tainted by present life circumstances.

Studies conducted in the late 1960s and early 1970s as veterans were returning home can say nothing about the long-term consequences of military service and of combat. Which of veterans' reentry problems would still be present a decade after their return home? Which would have been erased by time? These studies cannot say.

Many studies, especially those in the psychiatric literature, have been limited to small samples, often consisting of help-seeking veterans, those who have sought a counselor or hospital for help with a problem. Their findings cannot be generalized to veterans who have not sought help, either because they have not needed to, not wanted to, or not been able to.

On the other hand, studies of large, nationally representative groups of veterans and nonveterans have tended to restrict their analyses to data available from census tapes. These studies have been unable to look at the psychological consequences of military service because information on psychological well-being is not asked by the census. An exception is a large-scale study of Vietnam-era veterans and their peers conducted at the Center for Policy Research pursuant to Congressional legislation P.L. 95-202, the G.I, Improvement Act of 1977. This study by Egendorf, Kadushin, Laufer, Rothbart, and Sloan and their colleagues involved extensive interviews with 1,400 Vietnam-era veterans and their nonveteran peers. Adjustment of veterans in nine areas of life functioning was investigated: education, occupation, mental health, capacity to deal with stress, drug and alcohol abuse, arrests and convictions, marital status and satisfaction, friendship networks, and working through of the war experience. We will occasionally be comparing our findings with those obtained from this study.

Like the Egendorf et al. investigation, the present study overcomes limitations in earlier work on the Vietnam veteran by employing carefully chosen, nationally representative samples of Vietnam veterans, non-Vietnam veterans, and nonveterans. Our postservice data are not as comprehensive in scope as those of Egendorf and colleagues, having been collected from a relatively short (one-hour) mailed questionnaire instead of a lengthy (three- to five-hour) in-person interview. Our samples are, in a sense, not as comprehensive either, having been drawn from a single grade cohort; the Egendorf et al. samples are from men spanning the entire Vietnam-era generation. Our study, however, has two unique features that enable it to make a significant contribution to what is known about the precursors and aftermath of the Vietnam war for the soldiers involved. First, our study is a prospective one. Our data from veterans as well as nonveterans were gathered at three points in time, starting with the ninth grade (before any of the veterans had entered the service) and ending more than a decade after the veterans' return home from the war (when the men were thirty-six years old). Our preservice data are quite comprehensive, including background, ability, and psychological data gathered over a two-day period. We are thus in a good position to study the antecedents of Vietnam-era service, to describe in greater detail than previously possible what types of men served and what types avoided service. Second, we have been able to use our extensive preservice information to match the men in our three groups in terms of a host of early demographic, ability, and even psychological characteristics. Because of this research design, we have been able with relatively greater confidence than prior studies with more-limited preservice information to attribute group differences in our outcome variables to the military experience of the veterans instead of to different early, predisposing influences among the groups. We are thus in a better position than previously possible to call group differences in our outcome variables consequences of military service or of combat in the Vietnam era.

Selection of the Study Sample

The following steps were taken in selecting the participants in the current study and in collecting data from selected participants.

1. The men in the TALENT ninth-grade cohort were divided into two groups: (1) those who in 1974 reported that they had served or were currently serving on active military duty in the army, navy, air force, Marine Corps, or Coast Guard and (2) those who in 1974 reported that they had never served on active military duty.

2. A random sample of 1,385 veterans, representative of all veterans in group 1, was selected as the study's target-veteran sample.

3. A letter was sent to the 1,385 veterans in the target-veteran sample explaining the goals of this study, asking veterans to update the address Project TALENT had on file, and asking them whether they had ever served in Vietnam. (The existing TALENT file had information on whether the men had ever been in the military but not on where such service was spent.)

4. Two follow-up letters were sent to those who failed to respond to the first letter.

5. Intensive attempts were made to locate those who failed to respond to the three mailings. These efforts consisted of consulting telephone directories and information operators, writing to postmasters, checking Department of Motor Vehicles records, and calling parents, relatives, and former neighbors. The effort was quite successful. Of the 1,385 veterans in the target-veteran sample,

1,243 (90 percent) were located, 1,119 (81 percent) of whom had information regarding whether they had served in Vietnam. Seven veterans, located through their parents, were deceased; they were, of necessity, dropped from the study.

6. The 266 (19 percent) men in the original target-veteran sample who could not be located or for whom information on Vietnam service could not be obtained, and the seven deceased veterans, were replaced with other veterans. The replacements were chosen so as to match the originally chosen 266 non-respondents on over fifty key demographic, cognitive, and sociopsychological characteristics.

7. There were 599 Vietnam veterans and 786 non-Vietnam veterans in the final target-veteran sample (originals plus replacements). All 599 Vietnam veterans and a subset of 566 of the non-Vietnam veterans were chosen as potential study respondents.

8. A group of 830 nonveterans was then chosen from the same TALENT ninth-grade cohort to serve as the comparison group.

9. Intensive attempts were made to locate the 830 members of the target nonveteran sample. These attempts were similar in nature to those described for location of veterans in step 5. Six hundred sixty-seven of the 830 members of the nonveteran target sample (80 percent) were successfully located (three found to be deceased).

10. The survey questionnaire in appendix A was mailed to all located potential respondents (599 Vietnam veterans, 566 non-Vietnam veterans, and 667 nonveterans). The original mailing was followed by three other mailings, each three weeks apart, and by telephone calls to target respondents urging them to participate. We offered to interview by telephone those target respondents who did not want to take the time to fill out a pencil-and-paper questionnaire; fifteen respondents took us up on our offer.

11. In all, 481 Vietnam veterans, 502 non-Vietnam veterans, and 487 non-veterans returned a completed questionnaire, ten too late for inclusion in the data analysis. These numbers were 80 percent, 89 percent, and 73 percent of the respective located target groups to whom a questionnaire had been mailed. We are not sure why the questionnaire return rate for the nonveteran group was lower than that for the two veteran groups. Three explanations appear possible. (1) Our criterion for location was lower for the nonveteran group than for the veteran groups. For the latter groups (since we needed to know whether each man had served in Vietnam), we did not consider a man located until we had spoken in person to him or to a member of his household and obtained information on where he had served. For the nonveteran group, we considered a man located if an outside source—for example, a Department of Motor Vehicles representative or a telephone operator—could give us an address considered current. It is possible that some of these addresses were not really current and that some of our nonveterans never received the survey questionnaire at all. (2) The fact that we had personal contact with every veteran, or at least with a member of his household, prior to the mailing of the survey questionnaire

undoubtedly increased veterans' inclination to take the time to fill out the questionnaire. (3) Because the study was called a study of the personal consequences of military service in the Vietnam era, veterans had a greater personal stake in contributing to its success. Several nonveterans could not understand why a study like ours should include them since they had never served. Their puzzlement persisted even after we made numerous attempts to explain the importance of a control or comparison group. At any rate, the response rate figures obtained for each of the groups were acceptably, even impressively, high.

12. Two sets of weights were developed for each case in the final study sample. The first set made the Vietnam veterans, non-Vietnam veterans, and nonveterans in the study sample representative of all Vietnam veterans, non-Vietnam veterans, and nonveterans in the ninth-grade class of 1960. These weights were used for the analyses presented in chapter 2, which examines the antecedents of Vietnam-era service. The second set of weights made the non-Vietnam veterans and nonveterans similar to the Vietnam veteran group in terms of fifty-one preservice characteristics. These weights, producing the matched samples, were used for all analyses in chapters 3 through 6, which deal with the consequences of Vietnam-era service.

To assess the adequacy of the first (population) set of weights, we applied the set to our data and then compared our study sample's mean and standard deviation on two key variables—socioeconomic status and general academic aptitude—with corresponding weighted statistics obtained from the entire sample of 50,000 Project TALENT ninth-grade males. For our study sample of 1,470 men, the weighted mean and standard deviation on the socioeconomic status score were 96.37 and 10.70, respectively; for general academic aptitude, they were 434.31 and 115.5. TALENT population figures were 96.45, 10.49, 430.2, and 119.5. These figures show that our first set of case weights was successful in recapturing average population figures to within 0.03 standard deviation, an impressive accuracy level well within the range of acceptability for the current study.

To assess the adequacy of the second (matching) set of weights, we applied the set to our data and then compared the three study samples in terms of their mean scores on the fifty-one preservice characteristics given in table 1-1. There were no statistically significant differences on any of these variables. We conclude that our second set of case weights was successful in producing samples of Vietnam veterans, non-Vietnam veterans, and nonveterans well matched on early, preservice characteristics.

The Data

The initial Project TALENT tests, given to the men when they were in the ninth grade, at fourteen to fifteen years of age, consisted of: twenty-five tests of cognitive abilities, thirty-seven tests of knowledge in various fields, thirteen personality

Table 1-1
The Fifty-One Characteristics on which the Three Groups of Vietnam
Veterans, Non-Vietnam Veterans, and Nonveterans Were Matched

Sociodemographic characteristics
  Age in ninth grade
  Socioeconomic index
  Parents born in United States?
  Father's employer
  Father's military rank
  Father's military and veterans' activity
  Father's church or religious activity
  Parents' fluency in Oriental language
  Number of siblings
  Public versus private high school
  Size of high-school community
  High-school retention rate
  High-school curriculum (academic
  versus other)
  High-school curriculum (general versus
  college prep versus business versus
  vocational versus agriculture)

Cognitive characteristics
  Response credibility score[a]
  Screening score[a]
  General academic aptitude composite
  Mathematics test score
  Reading-comprehension test score
  Physical-science-information test score
  Mechanical-information test score
  Military-information test score
  Music-information test score
  Bible-information test score

Academic experiences
  High-school grades
  Study habits
  Leadership roles
  Membership in debating, dramatics, or
  music club
  Membership in military or drill unit
  Amount of extracurricular reading

Health characteristics
  Height
  Weight
  Self-rating of usual health
  Frequency of illness
  History of asthma

Educational characteristics
  Expected amount of education
  Amount of education desired by parents
  for self

Vocational characteristics
  Expected career
  Interest in physical sciences, engineering,
  and mathematics
  Interest in hunting and fishing
  Expected type of military service
  Preferred type of military service
  Reasons for preferred type of military
  service
  Perceived desirability of military career
  Interest in army officer career
  Interest in naval officer career
  Interest in Marine Corps officer career
  Interest in air force officer career
  Interest in military drill

Social and psychological characteristics
  Mature personality scale score
  Age on first date

Note: All characteristics used to match the samples were measured in 1960 when the men
were in the ninth grade.

[a] These scores reflect the extent to which subjects' responses were credible. A low score on
these scales reflects either failure to understand the test battery items or an inconsistent
pattern of responses indicative of a lack of seriousness about the test. Subjects failing to
meet a minimum cutoff score on these scales were eliminated from the data base.

scales, seventeen vocational-interest scales, a 394-item inventory of activities (for
example, membership in organizations, hobbies, study habits, schooling and
work-related activities), family and home characteristics, and plans for the future
in the areas of education, career, and military service.

The 1974 TALENT follow-up questionnaire survey, conducted when the men were twenty-nine to thirty years old, included items on educational experiences and plans, career-related experiences and plans, military service, if any, marriage and family life, and health and community activities.[3]

The survey questionnaire developed for the present study (see appendix A) was administered to the men in early 1981 when they were thirty-six to thirty-seven years old. It included items measuring the variables listed in table 1-2. The questionnaire was developed after a thorough review of the literature and included a wide range of constructs that had been linked, either theoretically or empirically, to military service. Prior to its being sent to members of the study sample, the questionnaire was reviewed by a panel of experts on military service and pretested on volunteer TALENT respondents who had not been chosen for the study sample of the present study.

Table 1-2
Variables Measured by Survey Questionnaire

	Group Asked These Questions			Questionnaire Item[a]	
Variables	Vietnam Veterans	Non-Vietnam Veterans	Nonveterans	Section Number	Item Number
Demographic background	x	x	x	I	A to I
Marriages and children	x	x	x	I	J to K
Educational history	x	x	x	I	L to N
Job history	x	x	x	I	O to AA
Financial situation	x	x	x	I	BB to GG
Physical health	x	x	x	II	A to M
Life satisfaction	x	x	x	III	A to B
Alienation	x	x	x	III	C
Social problems	x	x	x	III	D
Anxiety, depression, hostility	x	x	x	III	E
Brushes with the law	x	x	x	III	F to H
Personality traits	x	x	x	III	I
Organizational membership	x	x	x	III	J
Reason for not serving in military			x	III	K
Reason for serving in military	x	x		III	L
Military experiences	x	x		IV	A to L
Vietnam experiences	x			IV	M to W

[a]See appendix A.

Notes

1. In 1974, a survey questionnaire was mailed to the last-known addresses of the approximately 100,000 individuals who had originally participated in Project TALENT in 1960 as ninth graders. Available resources did not permit intensive efforts to locate and solicit the cooperation of all of these people. Therefore, a special sample of 4,779 individuals representative of the 100,000 was chosen in advance of the survey for intensive follow-up efforts, including telephone location and interviewing. In all, 3,863 (81 percent) of those in the special sample provided eleven-year follow-up data. For individuals not selected as part of the special sample, response rate to the mail questionnaire was much lower: 19,974, or 19.2 percent. Case weights for all respondents to the eleven-year follow-up have been computed to correct for attrition from 1960 to 1974; the weights give greater relative emphasis to data from the special sample. TALENT staff members have demonstrated the adequacy of these weights in several publications (Wise 1977; Abeles and Wise 1979–1980). It was this group of respondents to the TALENT ninth-grade eleven-year follow-up that formed the main sampling frame for the present Vietnam veteran study.

2. This chronology of major events comprising the Vietnam conflict was taken from *The Vietnam War*, edited by Ray Bonds (New York: Crown Publishers, 1979), pp. 12–14. © 1979 by Salamander Books Ltd.

3. Additional information on the Project TALENT data base can be obtained from *The Project TALENT Data Bank Handbook* by Wise, McLaughlin, and Steel (1979), available from the American Institutes for Research, P.O. Box 1113, Palo Alto, Calif. 94302 ($14.50).

2

Composition of the Vietnam-Era Force

Much discussion in the latter years of the Vietnam war and in the aftermath of the war has focused on the interrelated issues of who served in the military during this era, who would have served if there had been no draft, and who should serve in future times of national need. The draft, the all-volunteer force, and compulsory national service for all young Americans have been proposed, at various times, as the national policy that could best meet both the country's defense needs and young citizens' obligations to serve.

The Vietnam era was characterized by heavy conscription that started to gain momentum in 1965 and ended some two years before Gerald Ford's 1975 official presidential proclamation ending the Vietnam era. Critics of the draft have raised many concerns about the composition of the Vietnam-era force. First, it has been alleged, the unpopularity of the war placed a disproportionate share of the burden to serve on America's disadvantaged: blacks, the poor, and the academically disadvantaged were overrepresented in the military, despite the heavy draft that took place as the war progressed. A variant of this concern has centered on who, among those who did serve, actually fought the daily battles of the war. Again there has been the feeling that America's disadvantaged bore more than their fair share of the risks of combat. A final, related issue concerns the suspected particular unrepresentativeness of the white fighting force. While blacks who bore arms were representative of their fellow blacks, it is claimed, advantaged whites were greatly underrepresented in the Vietnam-era fighting force.

With the end of the Vietnam draft was born the present all-volunteer force, a new age in American military history in which the United States has maintained a large active-duty force of more than 2 million men and women without resort to conscription. Many of the same concerns about who served in Vietnam continue to be voiced about the present all-volunteer force.

These issues have captured serious attention both because of a violated sense of fairness and because America's survival as a military power is to some extent dependent on its increasingly sophisticated weapons and military technology being in capable hands.

This chapter investigates the legitimacy of these concerns. Based on the experience of the class of 1963, who did serve in the Vietnam era? Who among these men were sent to the Vietnam fire zone? Who among them saw combat? Were blacks and whites who served representative of fellow blacks and whites in their age group? If there had been no draft and the armed forces had been staffed solely by willing enlistees, who would have served?

In evaluating and interpreting the findings, the following limiting aspects of our study should be kept in mind. First, we will necessarily be talking about group findings; for example, we will be examining profiles of what the men who fought in Vietnam looked like (academically, socially, and psychologically), on the average, prior to their Vietnam stint. Clearly many individual Vietnam veterans will not have conformed to our average profile since an average is by definition a number made up of many individual scores—some below it, others above it.

Second, the findings are derived from and therefore limited to only one group of men: men who were in the ninth grade in 1960 and who for the most part graduated from high school in 1963, one year before the official start of the Vietnam era. One such grade group or grade cohort of men cannot stand for the entire Vietnam-era fighting force; the era spanned ten years and involved at least as many grade cohorts of soldiers. However, it is important to note that our study population is close to the average Vietnam-era veteran with respect to age; our men are only a half-year older (Veteran's Administration, *Age Distribution of Vietnam-Era Veterans,* 1979, p. 3).

The Vietnam war was not a homogeneous event. U.S. involvement in Vietnam rose gradually from 1962 through 1964, dramatically from 1965 through 1968, then declined slowly from 1969 through 1971, and dramatically thereafter (table 2-1). Public attitudes toward the conflict soured considerably after 1968. In general, previous studies have found that soldiers who came back to the United States before this date had fewer problems. They had been less exposed to drugs and to combat; the war was not as unpopular as it would later be; the economy was stronger and could absorb their reentry more easily. Because we are studying a single cohort, it is important to place the cohort in the context of this evolving historical event of interest. The last four columns of table 2-1 show how the service dates of men in the cohort were distributed over the war years. The modal (most-frequent) year of service exit was 1967, one year prior to the height of the fighting in 1968. This is in keeping with the slight upward age bias of the cohort, relative to other Vietnam-era soldiers. It is important to note, however, that the majority of the cohort's Vietnam veterans (70 percent) were still in the service as of 1968. A wide range of exit dates was represented among veterans in the cohort. Tables 2-2 and 2-3 show that a wide range of combat experiences was similarly represented.[1] In short, the men in this study cannot stand for all Vietnam-era soldiers; however, they are a very sensible cohort to study, and their experiences can shed light on many questions concerning the antecedents and consequences of Vietnam-era service and combat.

A final potential limitation of our study concerns the unique nature of the conflict. Vietnam was America's least-popular war, the only one the United States, in some sense, lost. One could question whether findings derived from

Table 2-1
Military-Service Dates, Class of 1963, in Relation to American Troop Strength in Vietnam

| | | Distribution of Military-Service Dates, Class of 1963 | | | |
| | | Vietnam Veterans | | Non-Vietnam Veterans | |
Year	Approximate Number of American Troops in Vietnam as of End of Year[a]	Percent Starting Service	Percent Ending Service	Percent Starting Service	Percent Ending Service
1962 and before	4,000	3.4	0.0	7.5	1.0
1963	15,000	16.5	0.0	20.4	4.4
1964	23,000	10.0	0.2	11.9	5.8
1965	181,000	24.7	1.7	21.7	7.1
1966	385,000	18.6	4.5	15.0	10.4
1967	486,000	12.6	23.2	7.1	26.2
1968	536,100	8.6	20.8	6.5	11.6
1969	474,000	4.6	17.4	4.6	11.1
1970	335,800	0.8	12.6	3.7	6.5
1971	200,000	0.0	5.1	0.7	5.1
1972	27,000	0.3	2.9	0.0	4.8
1973 and after	0	0.0	4.2	0.9	3.9
Still in service as of 1981		7.4		2.4	

[a] Adapted from Ray Bonds, ed., *The Vietnam War* (New York: Crown Publishers, 1979), pp. 12-14.

Table 2-2
Description of Combat Experiences of Vietnam Veterans, Class of 1963

| Combat-Experience Variables | Percent of Vietnam Veterans Experiencing Variable | | | | |
	Very Often	Often	Occasionally	Rarely, but at least once	Never
Receive fire from enemy	10.1	21.7	32.2	18.3	17.7
Fire own weapon at enemy	8.5	13.5	20.0	14.7	43.4
Kill enemy	5.3	7.7	11.7	12.3	63.0
See someone get killed	4.3	13.7	20.1	23.3	38.5
See enemy wounded	7.0	12.2	21.5	18.1	41.3
See American wounded	13.1	19.7	29.6	18.5	19.1
See enemy dead	9.7	12.0	24.2	17.5	36.7
See American dead	10.9	15.0	24.3	21.1	28.6
Find self in combat situation where survival was in jeopardy	5.7	8.1	17.5	32.4	36.2

Table 2-3

Distribution of Combat-Scale Scores, Vietnam Veterans, Class of 1963

Total Scale Score	Average Item Score	Interpretation of Score	Percent Vietnam Veterans in Category
9	1	Never experienced any combat behavior on list	12.7
10–18	1.1–2.0	On average, experienced behaviors rarely but at least once	35.9
19–27	2.1–3.0	On average, experienced behaviors occasionally	26.9
28–36	3.1–4.0	On average, experienced behaviors often	19.7
37–45	4.1–5.0	On average, experienced behaviors very often	4.8

such a unique period can be generalized outside the period. Yet we should not ignore the lessons of the Vietnam era. As a society, we can cope wisely with the future only if we examine and learn from the past.

What is important in evaluating results from a particular cohort and historical period is to keep the unique contextual aspects of the data in mind and to test the generality of findings across other cohorts and historical periods. We will do this, whenever possible, by comparing our results with those from other studies of the Vietnam-era soldier, as well as with more-contemporary data from the current all-volunteer force.

The Class of 1963: Who Served?

Figures 2-1 through 2-5 describe Vietnam veterans, non-Vietnam veterans, and nonveterans in the class of 1963 in terms of a wide range of demographic, cognitive, psychological, and vocational characteristics measured in 1960, when the men were in the ninth grade. The data in these figures are unique because of their comprehensiveness. Most other studies of the preservice characteristics of the Vietnam-era force and of the present all-volunteer force have been limited to in-depth descriptions of small, unrepresentative samples or to limited descriptions of larger, nationally representative samples (descriptions restricted to demographic characteristics such as race, socioeconomic status, and educational level). In contrast, our profiles portray a wide range of characteristics, including cognitive and psychological predispositions, generalizable to an entire cohort of men. All characteristics were measured prior to military service, when the men were about fifteen years of age, so we know that military service did not influence veterans' scores on the profiles. They are entry portraits, which will be supplemented by exit (postservice) portraits in subsequent chapters.

Descriptive information on a variety of characteristics is encompassed by the figures: demographic background (figure 2-1), academic aptitudes and achievements (figure 2-2), personality (figure 2-3), extracurricular activities while in the ninth grade (figure 2-4), and occupational interests (figure 2-5).

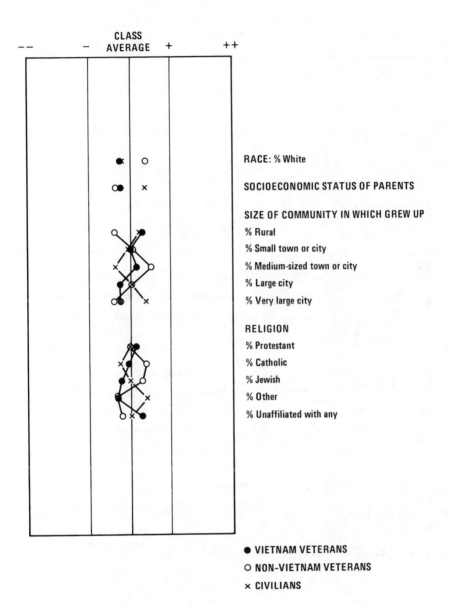

Figure 2-1. Demographic Profile of Vietnam Veterans, Non-Vietnam Veterans, and Nonveterans (Grade 9)

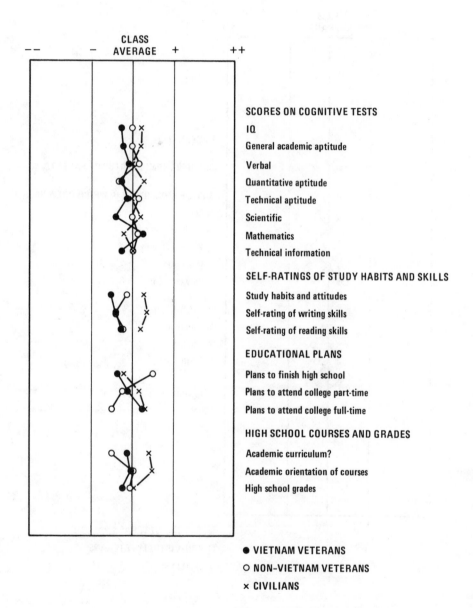

Figure 2-2. Academic Profile of Vietnam Veterans, Non-Vietnam Veterans, and Nonveterans (Grade 9)

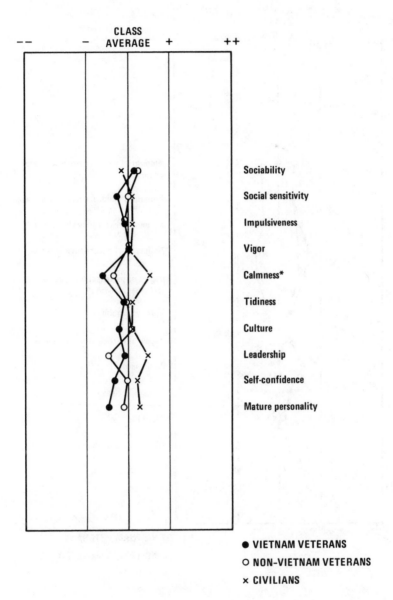

*Intergroup differences statistically significant at the 0.05 level.

Figure 2-3. Personality Profile of Vietnam Veterans, Non-Vietnam Veterans, and Nonveterans (Grade 9)

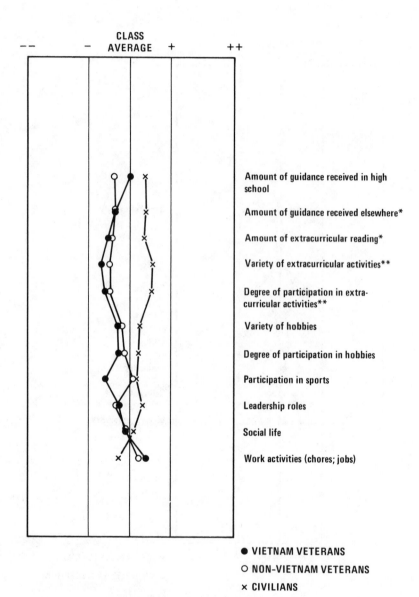

CLASS
--   -   AVERAGE   +   ++

Amount of guidance received in high school

Amount of guidance received elsewhere*

Amount of extracurricular reading*

Variety of extracurricular activities**

Degree of participation in extra-curricular activities**

Variety of hobbies

Degree of participation in hobbies

Participation in sports

Leadership roles

Social life

Work activities (chores; jobs)

● VIETNAM VETERANS
○ NON-VIETNAM VETERANS
× CIVILIANS

*Intergroup differences statistically significant at the 0.05 level.
**Intergroup differences statistically significant at the 0.01 level.

Figure 2-4. Preservice High-School (Extracurricular) Experiences of Vietnam Veterans, Non-Vietnam Veterans, and Nonveterans (Grade 9)

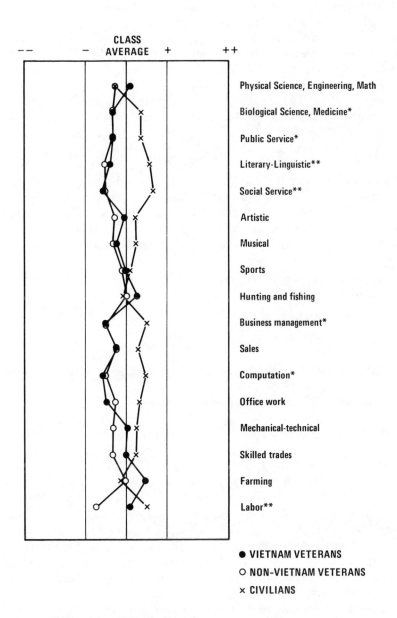

Figure 2-5. Vocational Interests of Vietnam Veterans, Non-Vietnam Veterans, and Nonveterans (Grade 9)

All profiles are presented in terms of each group's difference or deviation from the overall class average. Because the variables were measured on different scales, we have simplified the figures by presenting the deviations in terms of standard-deviation units. Points to the left of the center line indicate group scores lower than the overall class average and points to the right, higher. The vertical lines headed + and − represent differences of ±0.20 standard deviation in magnitude, a relatively small deviation. The vertical lines headed ++ and −− represent differences of ±0.50 standard deviation in magnitude, a moderate-sized deviation.

Because we analyzed data from only 500 men in each of the groups and did not poll all 1.1 million men in the study population, there is a margin of error in the figures. Statistical tests can be used to tell the probability that a given difference among our three groups, as portrayed in the figures, is real, as opposed to a chance difference that might not have been found if we had polled all 1.1 million men. A statistically significant finding means that there is less than a 5 percent probability that a difference as large as that found could have occurred by chance alone. We will use the following notation throughout the tables to indicate the probability that the reported difference among the three groups could have occurred by chance alone:

*Less than 0.05 (5 in 100).

**Less than 0.01 (1 in 100).

***Less than 0.001 (1 in 1000).

In short, the greater the number of asterisks attached to the finding, the greater our confidence in that finding.[2]

The groups of veterans and nonveterans are not as different from one another as popular belief might suggest. Not one of the group averages lies more than 0.2 standard deviation away from the overall class average. Statistical tests conducted to test the significance of obtained group differences confirm this conclusion. Of the demographic background differences portrayed in figure 2–1 (race, socioeconomic status of parents, size of community in which the individual grew up, and religion) and the academic aptitude and achievement differences portrayed in figure 2–2 (scores on eight cognitive tests, self-ratings of study habits and skills, educational plans, and high-school curriculum and grades) not one is statistically significant. The men who fought in Vietnam, the men who served in the military but were never sent to Vietnam, and their classmates who never served were rather similar regarding their family backgrounds, as well as their early academic abilities and achievements.

Figure 2–3 presents group profiles on ten personality traits: sociability, social sensitivity, impulsiveness, vigor, calmness, tidiness, culture, leadership, self-confidence, and mature personality. Only one significant difference emerged: in the ninth grade, the veteran groups, especially the Vietnam-veteran group, reported themselves as being less calm than did their classmates who never served.

A greater number of significant group differences was apparent in high-school extracurricular activities (figure 2-4) and early occupational interests (figure 2-5). In general, the two veteran groups had profiles more similar to each other than to the nonveteran group. Veterans had lower scores than their class-mates in amount of extracurricular reading (science, science fiction, plays, poetry, essays, classics, politics, world affairs, biography), variety of extracur-ricular activities, and degree of participation in these activities (school news-paper, school subject-matter clubs such as science and math clubs, debate, hobby clubs, farm-youth groups, church and neighborhood groups, political clubs, social clubs such as fraternities, military or drill units). Veterans in both groups expressed less interest in a whole gamut of occupational fields dealing with bio-logical science, medicine, public service, literary and linguistic matters, social service, business management, computation, and labor. They also reported having received less counseling outside their high school from parents, siblings, clergymen, friends, and unrelated adults.

The picture that emerges from the profiles presented in figures 2-1 through 2-5 is important: contrary to popular belief, those who served in the Vietnam era were comparable to those who did not serve in terms of early advantage in life (early indicators of success potential provided by racial and socioeconomic class and by academic abilities). Despite the fact that their social and academic positions were similar to those of their classmates, however, those who served— and especially those who served in Vietnam—appeared even at the early age of fifteen to be different in terms of personal self-concept, interests, and activities. They saw themselves as being less calm at this age than did their classmates who did not serve. They expressed fewer occupational interests and participated in fewer optional extracurricular activities. They also received less outside-school counseling than their classmates, although the data do not indicate whether this was because they spent less effort seeking it. In an era when military service was to become increasingly unpopular, the groups' early differences in behavioral and attitudinal indicators of control and efficacy may have spelled the differ-ence between service and escape from service.

Who Fought?

There were some psychological and behavioral differences between the men in the class of 1963 who served and those who did not; however, there were no significant demographic or academic differences between veterans and non-veterans. We now pursue the issue further by examining whether there were significant differences between those who fought and those who did not. Critics of the war have claimed that it was the socially deprived segments of American society who went to the battlefields to risk their lives. Did nonwhites, the poor, and the academically disadvantaged do more of the actual fighting of the Vietnam war than their socially and academically advantaged classmates? We address this question first by looking at the racial, socioeconomic, and academic aptitude composition of the U.S. ground forces—the army and Marine Corps—who, as table 2–4 shows, experienced more of the day-to-day fighting than the naval or air forces;[3] and second, by looking directly at racial, socioeconomic, and academic aptitude differences between Vietnam veterans who reported experiencing combat and those who did not.

Table 2–5 shows that there were significantly greater proportions of non-whites and men with lower-than-average socioeconomic status in the army and Marine Corps composed with other service branches. The percentage of men with lower-than-average academic aptitude was also higher in these ground forces, although the group difference did not reach statistical significance.

Table 2–6 lists nine combat-related experiences that Vietnam veterans might have had: receiving enemy fire, firing at the enemy, killing the enemy, seeing someone killed, seeing enemy wounded, seeing American wounded, seeing enemy dead, seeing American dead, and finding oneself in a life-threatening combat situation (Figley 1980).[4] White and nonwhite Vietnam veterans reported comparable amounts of exposure to these combat elements. Both rich and poor Vietnam veterans reported similar degrees of exposure. However, Vietnam veterans who had below-average academic aptitude scores in the ninth grade reported significantly more exposure than Vietnam veterans with above-average scores to four types of combat experiences: seeing enemy wounded,

Table 2–4
Combat Experiences of Men Stationed in Vietnam, Ground Troops versus Others

	Percent Vietnam Veterans Who Experienced This at Least Once		
Combat-Experience Variables	Men Who Served in Army and Marine Corps	Men Who Served in Navy, Air Force, and Coast Guard	Significance of Group Difference
Receive fire from enemy	91.9	65.4	***
Fire own weapon at enemy	68.8	34.7	***
Kill enemy	45.7	20.8	***
See someone get killed	68.9	47.9	***
See enemy wounded	70.2	37.9	***
See American wounded	88.6	67.1	***
See enemy dead	77.3	38.9	***
See American dead	77.6	59.9	**
Find self in combat situation where survival was in jeopardy	74.0	45.3	***

**Significant at 0.01 level.
***Significant at 0.001 level.

Table 2-5
Racial, Socioeconomic, and Academic Aptitude Composition of U.S.
Forces, Ground Troops versus Others

	Percent Who Served in Army and Marine Corps	Percent Who Served in Navy, Air Force, and Coast Guard
Race		
Whites	87.5	92.9
Nonwhites*	12.5	7.1
Socioeconomic status		
Above average	40.5	49.9
Below average*	59.5	50.1
Academic aptitude		
Above average	43.1	50.8
Below average	56.9	49.2

*Difference significant at 0.05 level.

Table 2-6
Racial, Socioeconomic, and Academic Aptitude Differences in Combat
Experiences, Vietnam Veterans

Combat Experience Variables	Percent Vietnam Veterans Who Experienced This at Least Once	Any Significant Differences in Percent Who Experienced?		
		Whites versus Nonwhites	High versus Low Socioeconomic Status	High versus Low Academic Aptitude
Receive fire from enemy	82.2	No	No	No
Fire own weapon at enemy	56.4	No	No	No
Kill enemy	37.5	No	No	No
See someone killed	61.3	No	No	No
See enemy wounded	58.5	No	No	Yes*
See American wounded	80.4	No	No	Yes*
See enemy dead	63.2	No	No	No
See American dead	70.6	No	No	Yes*
Find self in combat situation where survival was in jeopardy	63.7	No	No	Yes*

*A significantly higher proportion of Vietnam veterans with low academic aptitude experienced this, compared to Vietnam veterans with high academic aptitude.

seeing Americans wounded, seeing Americans dead, and finding oneself in a life-threatening combat situation. This increased risk on the part of men of lower-than-average academic ability was not brought about solely by the fact that a disproportionate number of them were enlisted men as opposed to officers. (Of the men with below-average academic scores, 73.1 percent were enlisted men; the comparable percentage for men with above-average scores was 60.3.) When the analysis is restricted to enlisted men in the Vietnam-veteran group and data from officers are eliminated, the significant academic aptitude differences between enlisted men who saw combat and those who did not persist.

In sum, although there were no significant differences in the demographic and ability profiles of the men in the class of 1963 who served in the Vietnam era and those who did not, there were significant differences between the men in the class who fought in this era and those who did not. Nonwhites and poor men were overrepresented in the army and Marine Corps, service branches that tended to engage in fighting; within the group of Vietnam veterans, men with lower-than-average academic abilities saw more combat than their brighter classmates.

Blacks and Whites in the Vietnam-Era Force

A final concern dealing with the issue of representativeness centers on the suspected underrepresentation of advantaged whites in the fighting force. While blacks who served were representative of their fellow blacks, it is claimed, whites who served were less advantaged than whites who did not. Table 2-7 presents the relevant findings from the class of 1963, separately for the two races. Two indexes of advantage are used: socioeconomic status of the man's parents and his own academic aptitude, both measured when he was in the ninth grade. Differences are examined for men who served in the armed forces versus those who did not; long termers, or those who served more than twenty-four months active duty, versus short termers, those who served twenty-four months or less; and willing enlistees versus other participants (men who either were drafted or who enlisted to avoid the draft).

In accordance with popular belief, blacks and whites who served were not similarly representative of their respective populations. Whites who served, and especially whites who enlisted willingly, came from significantly poorer families than whites who did not serve. In addition, whites who enlisted willingly had significantly lower academic aptitude than whites who did not (a rather large difference equivalent to about 0.40 standard deviation). Thus, the underrepresentation of advantaged whites in the Vietnam-era fighting force would have been even more severe without the draft.

In contrast, while there were no significant socioeconomic differences between blacks who served and those who did not, the former had significantly higher (0.56 standard deviation) academic aptitude. Blacks who served more than twenty-four months had especially high academic aptitude relative to other blacks. In short, the representativeness data for blacks fall in a direction opposite

Table 2-7
Extent to which Whites and Blacks Who Served in Armed Forces Were
Representative of All Whites and Blacks, Class of 1963

	Whites		Blacks	
	Mean (SD) Socio-economic Status	Mean (SD) Academic Aptitude	Mean (SD) Socio-economic Status	Mean (SD) Academic Aptitude
Total group (class of 1963)	97.2 (10.5)	447.4 (109.6)	88.1 (9.6)	302.7 (98.4)
Veteran status	*			*
Men who served in armed forces	96.4 (10.1)	439.8 (106.3)	89.6 (9.2)	328.8 (74.3)
Men who did not serve	98.2 (10.8)	455.9 (113.7)	87.3 (9.9)	280.6 (96.0)
Length of service				*
Over twenty-four months	96.5 (10.0)	447.2 (108.2)	87.9 (9.1)	348.6 (72.9)
Twenty-four months or less	95.9 (10.2)	434.2 (105.0)	91.3 (9.9)	297.1 (77.3)
Terms of enlistment	**	***		
Enlisted willingly	95.1 (10.0)	417.4 (96.9)	88.5 (8.8)	340.3 (52.7)
Did not enlist willingly	97.4 (9.9)	460.4 (110.1)	90.3 (9.8)	317.8 (94.1)

*Significant at 0.05 level.
**Significant at 0.01 level.
***Significant at 0.001 level.

to that for whites: brighter blacks were overrepresented in the Vietnam-era fighting force, possibly because, as other investigators have shown (Moskos 1973), preinduction examination requirements barred the lowest-scoring blacks from entering the service at all. In addition, the military has traditionally been an attractive career for blacks, who perceive more opportunities for advancement in the service than in civilian life (Card et al. 1975).

Summary and Comparison with Related Studies

Contrary to popular belief, there were no significant differences in the demographic background or academic abilities of the soldiers who were sent to Vietnam, the soldiers who were never sent to Vietnam, and their classmates who never served in the military. There were, however, some early psychological and behavioral differences among the three groups, with the veterans, and especially the Vietnam veterans, perceiving themselves at age fifteen as being less calm than their classmates, participating in fewer optional extracurricular activities at this age, expressing fewer occupational interests, and receiving less outside-school counseling than their classmates who never served.

There was some support for the popular belief that deprived segments of American society were disproportionately exposed to combat risks. Nonwhites and men of lower-than-average socioeconomic status were significantly over-represented among the ground troops (army and Marine Corps); whites and the better-off were overrepresented in the other branches of military service (navy, air force, Coast Guard) less exposed to combat risks. In addition, within the subgroup of Vietnam veterans, men of lower-than-average academic abilities reported more exposure to combat experiences than their brighter classmates.

There was strong support for the popular belief that advantaged whites were underrepresented among those who served on active military duty. In contrast, the blacks who served, and especially the blacks who served more than two years, were significantly brighter than their black classmates who did not serve.

How do these findings compare with available data from related studies? No other study has comparable preservice data on the academic aptitude, the personality traits, or the early high-school interests and behaviors of men who served versus their peers who did not. Therefore we cannot corroborate those of our findings dealing with these variables. However, there do exist several published studies on the demographic characteristics (race, socioeconomic status) of Vietnam-era veterans versus their peers. We will compare our findings with these data, an important exercise since our study is limited to one cohort of men. To the extent that our findings regarding the demographic profile of veterans and nonveterans are consistent with available findings from other studies, we can increase our confidence in the broad applicability of our full range of findings.

First, we examine what other investigators have found on the relation of race, military service, and combat in the Vietnam era. Moskos (1973) presents data showing that in 1972, the eighth year of the war, blacks constituted 11.1 percent of the U.S. armed forces, a figure roughly equivalent to the proportion of the U.S. population that was black. The study commissioned by Congress in 1977 (Kadushin, Boulanger, and Martin 1981, vol. 4) found that, consistent with our findings and contrary to popular belief, "almost equal proportions of blacks and whites went into the military and were stationed in Vietnam" (p. 502) and "an equal proportion of blacks and whites saw light combat" (pp. 498–499). "Twelve percent more blacks saw heavy combat, [though] this is not statistically significant" (p. 502). Fligstein (1980) studied a national sample of more than 25,000 men aged twenty-five through sixty-five in 1973, a sample that includes cohorts who served not just in Vietnam but in World War II and Korea as well. He found that over the last half-century, blacks have been less likely to serve in the military than whites. The consensus from all these studies appears to be well summarized by Moskos: in the Vietnam era, blacks were more likely to be drafted than whites because they were less likely to be in a position to obtain a deferment; however, a comparable proportion of blacks and whites actually served because blacks were four times more likely than whites to fail the preinduction mental and physical examinations. In the same era, blacks were slightly more exposed than whites to heavy combat, according to Kadushin's data as well as ours, but this difference was not large enough to reach statistical significance.

With respect to socioeconomic differences between Vietnam-era veterans and their peers, Fligstein found, consistent with our findings, that father's occupation (a commonly used index of family socioeconomic status) was not related to son's military participation. Also consistent with our findings, the Kadushin et al. study found no difference in the lower and lower-middle classes in the percentage of men who went into the military and those who remained civilians. However, Kadushin and his colleagues found that a much lower proportion of the upper class served. We reanalyzed our data on the relation between socioeconomic status and military participation, dividing our subjects into those in the upper class (more than one standard deviation above the mean) versus all others. We corroborated the Kadushin et al. finding of significantly lower service rates among the upper class.

Based on these comparisons, we have confidence in the accuracy and generalizability of our three findings. We can add one detail to make the relation between socioeconomic status and military participation more precise: there is a slight tendency for Vietnam-era veterans to come from poorer families than their classmates who never served (see figure 2-1). This difference is not statistically significant; however, when participation rates for upper class versus all other classes are studied, the difference reaches statistical significance, with significantly fewer members of the upper class having served in the military during the Vietnam era.

What the Picture Might Have Been without the Draft

There were interesting preservice psychological and behavioral differences between veterans and nonveterans in the class of 1963 but only negligible differences in the preservice demographic and ability profile of the groups. To some extent, the global representativeness of the military force was an artifact brought about by opposing forces: the better-off and brighter blacks were overrepresented among those who served, while comparable whites were underrepresented.

Larger deviations from representativeness were found in the demographic and ability composition of those who saw combat, with disadvantaged Americans reporting higher exposure to combat than their more-advantaged classmates.

We are now in a postconscription era, with an all-volunteer force. This historical turn of events makes it important to assess the extent to which the data on military participation during the Vietnam era might have been different without the draft. Table 2-8 shows that the roughly proportional allocation of minorities, poor, and not-so-bright among the three samples (Vietnam veterans, non-Vietnam veterans, and men who never served) probably would not have

Table 2–8
Extent of Coercion to Serve

Mode of Entry into Military Service	Race[a]		Socioeconomic Status**		Academic Aptitude***	
	Whites	Nonwhites	Higher than Average	Lower than Average	Higher than Average	Lower than Average
Drafted, served willingly	24.2%	34.1%	23.0%	27.0%	21.6%	28.2%
Drafted, served unwillingly	2.1	1.7	2.8	1.4	2.1	2.0
Enlisted willingly	48.6	53.6	43.6	53.4	40.4	56.4
Enlisted unwillingly (to avoid the draft)	16.9	10.0	19.8	13.4	25.9	8.2
Other	8.2	0.6	10.7	4.8	9.9	5.2

[a] Difference in distributions barely missed being significant at 0.05 level (there is a 0.07 probability that the distribution difference occurred because of chance).
**Difference in distributions significant at 0.01 level.
***Difference in distributions significant at 0.001 level.

been achieved without the draft. Nonwhites, men with lower-than-average socio-economic status, and men with lower-than-average academic aptitude character-ized themselves as being willing draftees and especially willing enlistees (they would have enlisted even if they were not in danger of being drafted) to a sig-nificantly greater extent than their more-advantaged classmates. The Vietnam-era draft may not have been the perfect equalizer; undoubtedly the truly ad-vantaged were able to avoid being drafted. These data do show, however, that the draft made a significant contribution toward more-representative service on the part of all segments of American youth.

This conclusion is supported by data on the composition of the post-Vietnam all-volunteer force. The trend since the end of the draft through the end of the 1970s has been downward in terms of both sociodemographic status and mental-aptitude level, especially for the army and Marine Corps ground forces (Janowitz and Moskos 1979).

Notes

1. These combat behaviors were taken from the work of Charles Figley and his colleagues at Purdue University (Figley 1980). The behaviors form a combat-intensity scale, which had a coefficient alpha reliability of 0.91 in Figley's 1977 study of 626 American Legion veterans (Figley, personal communication, 1980). A similar coefficient alpha was obtained in the present study: 0.92. The be-haviors obviously form a homogeneous set of items. The total combat score, when used (as it will be in subsequent chapters), is obtained by summing scores from the nine component items. Each item is scored on a five-point scale, with a

1 standing for "never" (experienced this behavior), a 2 for "rarely, but at least once," 3 for "occasionally," 4 for "often," and 5 for "very often." Possible combat scores could thus range from 9 (no combat experience whatsoever) to 45 (extremely intense combat experience). For the Vietnam veterans in the present study, the range of actual combat scores spanned the entire theoretical range 9 to 45, with a mean of 22.15 and a standard deviation of 11.74.

2. Statistical significance was always assessed using effective sample size as opposed to raw or actual sample size. Effective sample size refers to the number of equally weighted cases that would be required to obtain a level of accuracy equal to the level achieved with differentially weighted cases. It is the appropriate sample size to use in evaluating the statistical significance of findings obtained with weighted data, as all our findings were. In the present study, effective sample size was 750 for analyses in the present chapter using population weights and 998 for analyses in the next four chapters using matching weights.

3. See note 1.

4. See note 1.

3 Schooling Patterns

Overview of Analytic Issues and Procedures

Chapter 2 presented a detailed description of Vietnam veterans, non-Vietnam veterans, and nonveterans from the class of 1963 in the ninth grade. They were about fifteen years old at that time, and none of them had as yet experienced life in the military. The point of the chapter was to paint entry or preservice portraits of the three groups.

This and the next three chapters, in contrast, paint exit portraits. They present data on the education, work, family, and personal lives of the men at age thirty-six when almost all of them were again civilians. To the extent possible, experiences both during and after military service are described in order to give a progressive picture of the men's development with time and age. In this and the next three chapters, we attempt to attribute differences among the three groups to military service in general or to military service in a war zone in particular. Thus it is important that earlier (premilitary service) differences among the groups be taken into consideration. Otherwise postservice differences could very well be due to the fact that the men in the three groups were different to begin with. In this and the next three chapters, we have therefore used a second set of case weights, different from that used in chapter 2. This new set of weights makes the three groups comparable in terms of fifty-one sociodemographic, cognitive, academic, health, educational, vocational, and sociopsychological characteristics measured in the ninth grade. Table 1-1 listed these fifty-one characteristics. They were chosen from among the variables measured by Project TALENT when the men were fifteen years old. The choice was based on a review of the literature on the precursors of our outcome variables of interest: educational attainment, occupational attainment, physical and psychological health, and satisfaction with family and personal life. Because the groups have been matched on the fifty-one characteristics listed in table 1-1, we can rule out those characteristics as being the cause of group differences documented in this and the next three chapters.

It is important to keep in mind, however, that the non-Vietnam veteran and nonveteran comparison groups will henceforth be matched with the Vietnam-veteran group and will therefore no longer be representative of their respective populations. As a consequence, we should not expect the present and subsequent chapters' data from these two comparison groups to dovetail with data from other studies not using similarly matched samples. What is important for our purpose is the relative position of the three samples on our outcome variables. Given similar early characteristics, are the samples comparable at age thirty-six? If the answer is yes (a statistical test shows no significant difference among the three samples' scores), we have strong reason to believe that military service did not affect the outcome variable. If the answer is no (there is a statistically significant difference among the three samples' scores), we conclude that it is likely that military service had an effect. We examine the magnitude of the effect and occasionally conduct further analyses to try to account for large effects and for all effects forming a consistent pattern.

A further question of interest centers on the impact of the Vietnam experience itself on the outcome variables. If there is a significant difference among the three samples on a particular outcome variable, is the difference attributable to the general military experience of the two veteran samples or to the more-particular Vietnam-related experience of the group of Vietnam veterans? We arrive at an answer to this question in the following way. First, we examine whether the average score or the distribution of scores of the non-Vietnam veteran group on the outcome variable is closer to the corresponding data for the nonveteran group or for the Vietnam-veteran group. If the non-Vietnam-veteran score or distribution is significantly different from that of the civilian group but not significantly different from that of the Vietnam-veteran group, this is a clue that perhaps the general military experience caused the initially obtained overall significant difference among the three samples. To the extent that a similar pattern is found for other outcome variables conceptually related to the one of interest, we have even greater faith in this conclusion. On the other hand, if the non-Vietnam-veteran score is similar to that of the nonveteran group but significantly different from that of the Vietnam-veteran group, this is an indication that something unique about the Vietnam experience caused the overall difference among the three groups.

Our first hypothesis is that this unique experience is combat. We test this hypothesis by examining whether, within the sample of Vietnam veterans, the score on the outcome variable is significantly associated with the intensity of the combat experienced. If it is, and if we can rule out other potentially spurious causes of the association, we have good reason to believe that the trauma of combat made an impact on the outcome variable. If it is not, we have to search for other explanations; perhaps the relatively harsher homecoming given the Vietnam veterans caused them to be different from other veterans of their age at midlife. The present study, however, lacks good data on various characterizations of the homecoming so we cannot pursue homecoming-related explanations with the rigor we would have wanted. (We do have information on when the homecoming occurred that can be used as a weak proxy for favorableness of the reception accorded the Vietnam veteran upon reentry: public attitudes toward the war and its soldiers soured considerably after 1968.)

Schooling Patterns, Ages Sixteen through Thirty-Six

The few available studies on the educational consequences of military service in the Vietnam era have had one or both of the following goals: to document differences in the number of years of schooling attained by veterans versus nonveterans at a certain time or a certain age and to account for these group differences by linking educational achievement to the military experience or to preexisting differences between veterans and nonveterans (Fligstein 1980; Rothbart, Sloan, and Joyce 1981).

The general finding is that a greater proportion of veterans have high-school degrees; however, a greater proportion of nonveterans have college degrees. Given that more than seventy percent of all veterans resume their educational careers following their military stint (Rothbart, Sloan, and Joyce 1981), it is not surprising that the magnitude of the educational difference varies from study to study, as a function of when the educational snapshot was taken: the later in the life course, the smaller the difference.

This portion of our study attempts to contribute to what is known about the educational consequences of military service in several ways. First, we present more than just a snapshot of the groups' educational achievement at a single point; rather, we attempt to give a changing picture of the groups' educational progress from age sixteen through age thirty-six. Second, the veteran and nonveteran groups are matched in terms of fifty-one preservice sociodemographic, cognitive, academic, health, educational, vocational, and sociopsychological characteristics. We can more accurately attribute observed postservice group differences to the military experience of the veterans, as opposed to preservice differences between veterans and nonveterans. Finally, we present the data on the matched groups' educational progress separately by degree. Interesting results emerge that would not have been detected if we had merely charted progress on the gross index of years of education received. There are differences from degree to degree in the educational catching up done by veterans. The veteran groups start out with a higher percentage of high-school degrees received on time (in 1963). With the passage of time, this gap in favor of veterans with high-school degrees widens. In addition, veterans catch up and eventually surpass their nonveteran classmates on the lower-level post-high-school vocational and two-year college (A.A.) degrees. In contrast, by age thirty-six veterans have not caught up with their nonveteran classmates on the higher-level college and post-college degrees. It is likely that they never will.

We turn now to the data, which will present these findings in greater detail.

On-Time versus Off-Time Educational Careers

The percentage of matched Vietnam veterans, non-Vietnam veterans, and nonveterans who received a high-school, vocational, A.A., four-year college, masters, or doctoral degree on time is given in table 3-1. *On time* is defined as the year men in this cohort would have received the various degrees if they had continued their high-school and post-high-school educational careers without interruption and full time, or close to full time. Because all of the subjects were in grade 9 in 1960, they should have received their high-school degree in 1963 and, for those who elected to take a noncollege vocational-training route, a vocational degree by 1966. Those entering college should have received the Associate of Arts or two-year college degree by 1966, the bachelors or four-year college degree by 1968, their masters degree by 1970, and their doctoral (Ph.D. or equivalent) degree by 1972.

There were significant differences in the extent to which men in the three matched groups were able to receive the various degrees on time. A greater proportion of veterans than nonveterans received their high-school degree on time. This is in keeping with findings from other studies showing that "high school graduates were most likely to serve in Vietnam" (Fligstein 1980, p. 305). In contrast, a higher proportion of nonveterans received the higher-level (college, masters, Ph.D.) degrees on time. This is not surprising because for a majority of veterans in this cohort, military service was the primary force interrupting continuous schooling. Consistent with this fact, the Fligstein study found that next to the group of high-school graduates, those with less than a high-school education were most likely to have served in Vietnam. In addition, and consistent with our findings, "college attendance had a strong [negative] effect on whether one served, and those who went to college . . . served even less frequently than those with no education" (Fligstein 1980, p. 305).

By 1981, a decade or so after the veterans' miliary service, they had successfully reduced some of the educational differences between themselves and their nonveteran high-school classmates. Significantly higher proportions of veterans than nonveterans have high-school, vocational, and A.A. degrees. Proportioately more nonveterans than veterans continue to have the higher-level degrees (four-year college, masters, Ph.D.), but only the group difference for the Ph.D. degree is statistically significant.

Subtracting the on-time from the corresponding 1981 percentages (table 3-1) yields the approximate percentage of each group receiving each of the various degrees off-time. These indicate a return to school after education was interrupted.

Veterans returned to school and completed a degree program to a greater extent than did nonveterans. This was true for all of the degrees examined except for the masters and Ph.D. degrees. One or both of the following explanations could account for the continuing deficit of masters and doctoral degrees in the veterans groups. First, veterans may not yet have had enough time to complete their full schooling agenda. Some did not return to civilian life until the early and middle 1970s. They may have had high-school and college degrees to complete before they could begin even to consider these postcollege degrees.

Table 3-1
Percentage in Each Study Group Receiving Various Degrees by 1981

Degree	On Time[a]				By 1981				Off-Time[b]		
	Vietnam Veterans	Non-Vietnam Veterans	Non-veterans	Is Group Difference Significant?	Vietnam Veterans	Non-Vietnam Veterans	Non-veterans	Is Group Difference Significant?	Vietnam Veterans	Non-Vietnam Veterans	Non-veterans
High school	83.7	83.5	75.0	Yes**	94.9	96.2	84.7	Yes***	11.2	12.7	9.7
Vocational	7.2	6.9	5.5	No	23.3	21.7	11.5	Yes****	16.1	14.8	6.0
A.A.	4.3	2.4	6.6	Yes*	19.2	12.2	9.8	Yes**	14.9	9.8	3.2
College (four-year)	10.9	11.1	21.6	Yes***	26.2	28.3	31.8	No	15.3	17.2	10.2
Masters	0.9	0.7	5.2	Yes****	8.7	8.7	12.9	No	7.8	8.0	7.7
Ph.D.	0.0	1.3	2.6	Yes*	1.8	2.8	5.4	Yes*	1.8	1.5	2.8

[a]Refers to the year the degree would have been received if the subject had not had any educational interruptions. For our cohort of men who were in the ninth grade in 1960, we define on-time as follows for various degrees: high school, 1963; vocational, 1966; A.A., 1966; college (four-year), 1968; masters, 1970; and Ph.D., 1972.
[b]Defined as any year between the on-time year given in note a and 1981.

*Significant at the 0.05 level.
**Significant at the 0.01 level.
***Significant at the 0.001 level.

Possibly veterans will catch up with their nonveteran classmates on these higher-level degrees, as they did with the lower-level degrees. Second, college-trained veterans may not be very interested in pursuing higher degrees, either because they hold different career interests from their nonveteran classmates or because by the time they get to these postcollege transition points, they are quite far along their life course, in terms of age as well as family responsibility. They likely have families and may view pursuit of a postcollege degree at this late stage as not being worth the trouble or investment.

Whatever the reason, our findings are again consistent with others on the careers held by veterans versus nonveterans. Rothbart and his colleagues (1981) found that "college-trained veterans, though they hold relatively high level jobs, are less likely to hold professional and technical jobs and more likely to hold managerial jobs than similarly trained non-veterans" (p. 123). This is what one would expect if college-trained veterans failed to pursue more-specialized (professional and technical) postcollege education. Of course, it is also possible that military service itself prepares one for managerial-type jobs.

Pacing of Educational Development

Figures 3-1 through 3-6 present a more-detailed picture of the groups' educational progress in the years 1963 through 1981. The figures show more clearly the educational pacing and development of the three groups of men. Figure 3-1 shows how the veteran groups start off with a significantly greater proportion of high-school graduates than does the nonveteran group. The gap widens slightly with time as the veterans return to civilian life and an even greater proportion of them complete high school.

Figure 3-2 shows that as of 1966, the on-time year for completion of a vocational degree, roughly the same proportions of men in the three matched groups hold such a degree. Starting about 1969, however, two years after most veterans in the class began their return to civilian life, increasing proportions of veterans compared to nonveterans complete vocational training. The gap widens steadily until about 1978, when the difference appears to stabilize with a 10 percent difference in favor of the veteran groups (roughly 20 percent of veterans and 10 percent of nonveterans with a vocational degree).

Figure 3-3 depicts the pacing of the three groups' receipt of the A.A. degree. The figure exhibits interesting similarities and differences when compared with pacing data for the other degrees. As with the other degrees, the nonveterans' curve reaches its maximum value in the on-time year, 1966, much earlier than the veteran curves. The veterans lag behind until 1970, three years after the modal (most-frequent) year of exit from the military (1967). By 1970, the veterans have caught up with their classmates as far as proportions holding the A.A. degree are concerned. Unlike the other figures, however, figure 3-3 shows

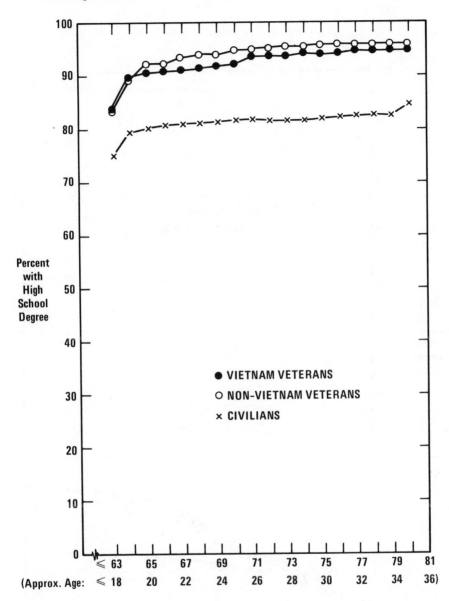

Figure 3–1. Pacing of Receipt of High-School Degrees for Three Study Groups,
1963–1981

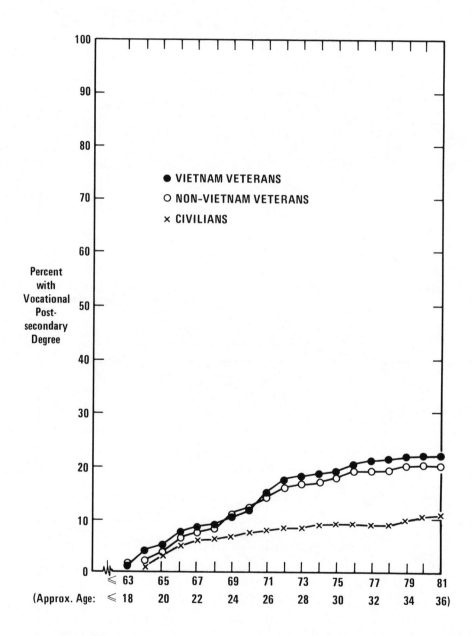

Figure 3-2. Pacing of Receipt of Vocational Degrees for Three Study Groups, 1963–1981

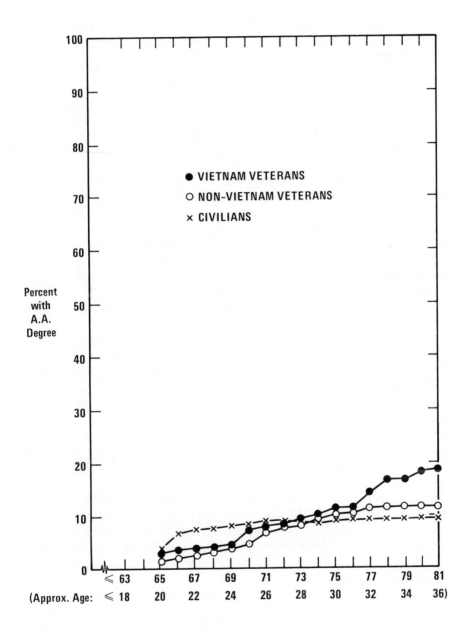

Figure 3-3. Pacing of Receipt of A.A. Degrees for Three Study Groups, 1963–1981

the Vietnam-veteran group diverging from the non-Vietnam veteran and the nonveteran groups, starting in 1977. By 1981, the latest available point in our study, there are almost twice as many Vietnam veterans as non-Vietnam veterans or nonveterans with the A.A. degree. Why this is so is unclear. One could speculate that the greater long-term adjustment difficulties experienced by the Vietnam veterans (see chapter 5), coupled with the financial attraction of GI bill educational benefits, may have caused them to seek refuge in the relatively more-sheltered environment of school, following either a period of unemployment or of work. This explanation is also consistent with our findings regarding the persistence of work-related problems and deficits on the part of the Vietnam veterans.

Like the other figures, figure 3–4 shows that the nonveterans have finished their college education at an earlier point in their life than the veterans. By 1974, almost all of the nonveterans who will ever get a college degree have gotten it. (Note, though, that 1974 is considerably later than the on-time year of 1968, indicating that even in the nonveteran group, many intersperse going to college with working.) In contrast, the veteran curves do not peak until around 1978–1979. By 1981, it appears that all three curves have stabilized, with the nonveteran group having the highest proportion of college graduates (approximately 32 percent), followed by the non-Vietnam-veteran group (approximately 28 percent), and lastly by the Vietnam-veteran group (approximately 26 percent). These differences are not statistically significant.

The story for the pacing of the masters degree (figure 3–5) is similar to that for the college degree, with the exception that the curves for the two veteran groups are more similar than they were for the college degree; also, they may not have stabilized by 1981. The difference in 1981 between the proportion of veterans and nonveterans with a masters degree is not significant. This, coupled with the fact that the veteran curves may still be rising, indicate that the final position of the three groups relative to masters degrees is still somewhat in doubt. The figure would suggest, though, that there will continue to be more nonveterans than veterans with masters degrees among samples matched for preservice characteristics.

This final relative advantage of the nonveteran group over the veteran groups can be predicted with even more certainty for the Ph.D. degree. All of the curves in figure 3–6 seem to have stabilized by 1974. The difference among the proportions in each group with a doctoral degree in 1981 (5.4 percent for the nonveterans, 2.8 percent for the non-Vietnam veterans, 1.8 percent for the Vietnam veterans) is statistically significant.

Summary

By the time they have reached age thirty-six, our matched groups of veterans and nonveterans have acquired roughly the same average number of years of

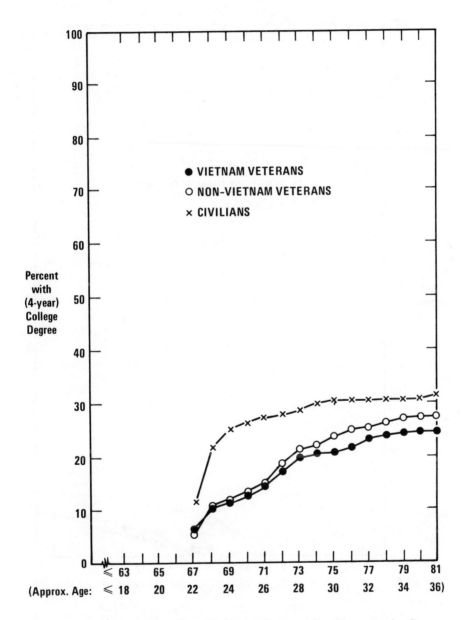

Figure 3–4. Pacing of Receipt of College Degrees for Three Study Groups,
1963–1981

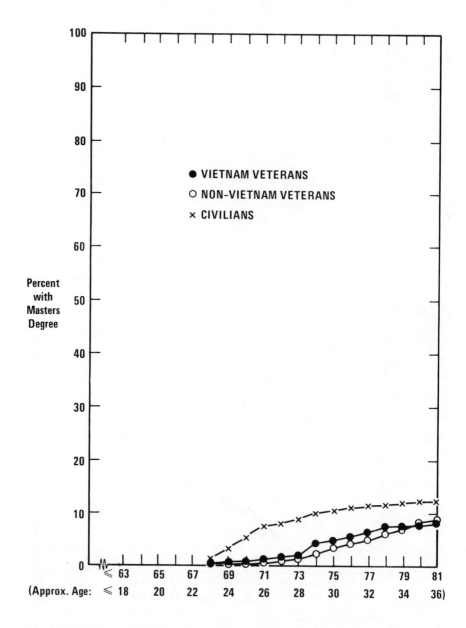

Figure 3-5. Pacing of Receipt of Master's Degrees for Three Study Groups, 1963–1981

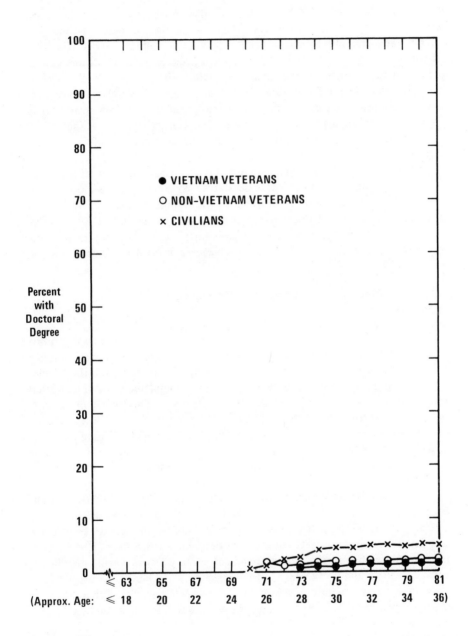

Figure 3–6. Pacing of Receipt of Doctoral Degrees for Three Study Groups, 1963–1981

schooling, but there are important differences in the patterning and pacing of their accomplishments. The nonveterans' educational careers have been less severely interrupted; the nonveterans tend to get their degrees on time. The veterans' educational careers have been interrupted by military service. The high-school period does not appear to have been affected to a significant extent; proportionately more veterans than nonveterans finish high school on time, indicating that their military service came after high school. After leaving the service, veterans catch up to and even surpass their classmates with respect to proportions completing vocational and two-year college degrees, but they fail to catch up with their classmates with respect to college and especially postcollege degrees.

Do the educational consequences of military service differ according to race, academic aptitude, and socioeconomic status? Who benefits the most, educationally, from military service? Conversely, who is most harmed? In the interest of simplicity, we restrict the analyses that follow to consequences for the number of years of schooling obtained by age thirty-six. We do not examine subgroup differences in the year-by-year pacing of receipt of the various degrees.

Subgroup Differences in the Educational Consequences of Military Service

Three statistical analyses of variance (ANOVAs) were conducted to determine to what extent individual differences in educational attainment were attributable to the men's veteran status, their race, their academic abilities, and their socioeconomic origins. In each analysis, the number of completed years of education reported by the men in the 1981 survey was treated as the dependent variable, or the variable to be accounted for. The independent variables, those hypothesized to account for differences in years of schooling completed, varied from one analysis to the next. In the first, the independent variables were veteran status and race; in the second, veteran status and academic aptitude; in the third, veteran status and socioeconomic status of the man's parents.

Each analysis yielded answers to two sets of questions: Could differences in years of schooling completed be accounted for by differences in the men's veteran status, race, academic aptitude, or socioeconomic status? Were there significant interaction effects between the independent variables? That is, were the educational bonuses and disadvantages of military service equally distributed between whites and nonwhites, and among men of higher-than-average versus lower-than-average socioeconomic status and academic ability? Table 3–2 summarizes the answers to these questions. We address the first question first.

Main Effects

The relation between veteran status and eventual (as of age thirty-six) educational attainment was not statistically significant. The men in the three groups

Table 3–2
Effect of Veteran Status Group, Race, Academic Aptitude, and
Socioeconomic Status on Years of Education Received by 1981:
Vietnam Veterans, Non-Vietnam Veterans, and Nonveterans

Factor Hypothesized to Influence Years of Education	Was Factor Significantly Related to Years of Education?	What Was Nature of Significant Relationship?
Main effects		
Veteran status group[a]	No	
Race[b]	No	
Academic aptitude[c]	Yes***	Those with above-average academic aptitude had two more years education than those with below-average academic aptitude
Socioeconomic status[c]	Yes***	Those with above-average socioeconomic status had 1.22 more years education than those with below-average socioeconomic status
Interaction effects		
Group x race	No	
Group x academic aptitude	No	
Group x socioeconomic status	Yes***	Military service was especially helpful for the educational development of individuals of low socioeconomic status (SES): Veterans of low SES had a half-year more education than civilians of low SES In contrast, veterans of high SES had a half-year less education than civilians of high SES

Source: Data obtained from three ANOVAS, all of which used years of education reported in the 1981 survey as dependent variable. The independent variables in the first ANOVA were veteran status group and race. The independent variables in the second ANOVA were veteran status group and academic aptitude score in 1960. The independent variables in the third ANOVA were veteran status group and parents' socioeconomic status, as reported in 1960.

[a]There were three matched veteran status groups: Vietnam veterans, non-Vietnam veterans, and nonveterans.

[b]There were two racial categories: white and nonwhite.

[c]There were two academic aptitude and two socioeconomic status categories: above average (for the class) and below average.

***Significant at the 0.001 level.

had completed roughly the same number of years of schooling by age thirty-six: 13.6 to 13.8 years (approximately 1.7 years beyond the 12 years required to get a high-school diploma). This finding is not surprising because the groups were matched in terms of characteristics as of grade 9. The finding means that the groups were able to turn their similar potential into similar educational achievement. Service in the military or in Vietnam did not hamper the two veteran groups, at least with respect to the number of years of schooling completed by age thirty-six. (But recall that enormous differences did exist between the three matched groups in terms of when and where the educational investment was made: in noncollege vocational or in college training. An average index taken at one point, such as number of years of schooling completed as of age thirty-six, masks these crucial facts.)

Table 3–2 also indicates that the relation between race and years of education was not statistically significant. Whites and nonwhites in the matched samples had completed roughly the same number of years of school by age thirty-six: 13.68 and 13.55, respectively. To interpret this finding correctly, it is important to recall two special facts about the study design: the whites and nonwhites in the non-Vietnam-veteran and nonveteran groups were chosen to look like the whites and nonwhites in the Vietnam-veteran group, and the data presented in chapter 2 showed that white and black veterans were not representative of all whites and all blacks in their age group: white veterans came from poorer families and were less bright that whites in general, whereas black veterans tended to be richer and brighter than their fellow blacks. These facts indicate that the whites and blacks in the matched samples were more similar to one another, both sociodemographically and academically, than whites and blacks in the general population. For such racial subgroups with similar early advantage, the ability to translate potential into educational achievement is roughly equivalent. There were no statistically significant differences in the number of years of schooling attained by whites and nonwhites in the three groups by age thirty-six.

Although race was not a significant factor in determining educational achievement once other indicators of early advantage were controlled, academic ability clearly was. We divided the men in the three samples according to whether their academic aptitude test scores in grade 9 were above or below the class mean. By age thirty-six, the former group had completed an average of 14.77 years of schooling and the latter an average of only 12.79 years. This difference of two years was highly significant.

Similarly socioeconomic status of the man's family of origin was significantly related to educational achievement at age thirty-six, though not as strongly as academic ability was. Above-average socioeconomic status produced an average of 14.30 years of schooling by age thirty-six and below-average status an average of 13.08 years.

These findings can be summarized by saying that when carefully chosen, matched samples of Vietnam veterans, non-Vietnam veterans, and nonveterans are studied, socioeconomic status of the family of origin and especially academic ability have strong impact on later educational achievement; however, neither military service, whether in or out of a war zone, nor race has a significant impact on years of schooling completed by age thirty-six. No one would contest the accuracy of the first finding. But data from other studies appear, at first glance, to contradict the second finding. For example, Rothbart and colleagues

(1981) found that nonveterans are better educated than non-Vietnam veterans who, in turn, are better educated than Vietnam veterans. They also found that this educational deficit on the part of veterans remained even after statistically controlling for eight factors other than veteran status: father's occupation, mother's employment status, race, current age, age at entry into the military, area of residence, number of siblings, and the early (preservice) educational attainment of the respondent himself. Consistent with our findings, Rothbart and colleagues found that the educational deficit on the part of veterans does not appear in the black subgroup: "black veterans . . . are better educated than black nonveterans" and "the educational gap separating white and black veterans is less than that separating white and black nonveterans." However, seemingly contrary to our second finding, they also found that "white veterans are better educated than black veterans" (p. 123).

In reconciling our findings with those obtained by Rothbart and his colleagues, it is important to note that Vietnam-veteran, non-Vietnam-veteran, and nonveteran samples of Rothbart and colleagues were not matched on preservice characteristics, whereas our three samples were. Moreover, their samples spanned a wide age range; our samples were restricted to men belonging to a single age (more precisely, grade) cohort. In some of their analyses of veterans' versus nonveterans' educational attainment, Rothbart and colleagues did statistically control for eight preservice characteristics. However, such statistical control does not achieve cross-sample comparability to the same extent that matching on fifty-one preservice characteristics does. The authors acknowledge this: "If the relationship [between the military experience and subsequent educational attainment] persists [subsequent to statistical controls], we can only assume that we have failed to prove the hypothesis of spuriousness. There may be other factors that we have not tested that might explain away the observed relationship" (p. 245). The wide age range of the Rothbart and colleagues samples also makes their study quite different from ours, especially in light of our finding that the pacing of educational development is very different for veterans and nonveterans. The yearly education increments are not constant for either the veteran or nonveteran group, so statistically controlling for age the way Rothbart and colleagues do does not make their sample comparable to ours.

In the light of all this, what conclusions can we make with confidence? Academic ability and socioeconomic status play a large role in determining subsequent number of years of schooling obtained; military experience plays a relatively smaller role. While black veterans get more years of schooling than black nonveterans, this is because the former had higher potential to begin with (being, on the average, brighter and richer; also, even prior to service entry, more of the former had high-school diplomas). Again, there is no evidence that military service makes a difference in terms of ultimate number of years of schooling completed.

We pursued this conclusion further by examining whether, within the group of Vietnam veterans, those who saw heavy combat (those scoring in the top third of the combat scale) subsequently achieved different levels of schooling from those who engaged in no or only light combat. We found no evidence that combat intensity makes a difference in terms of ultimate number of years of schooling completed. The heavy-combat group reported having completed 13.83 years of schooling by age thirty-six; the no- or light-combat group reported having completed 13.70 years of schooling by the same age. This difference was not statistically significant.

Interaction Effects

Were there significant interactions between veteran status on the one hand, and race, academic ability, or socioeconomic status on the other? Did military service differentially affect the educational achievement (as of age thirty-six) of whites versus nonwhites, the bright versus the less bright, and the rich versus the poor? The first two interactions were not statistically significant; the educational consequences of military service were similar for whites and nonwhites and for those of above-average and below-average academic ability. The third interaction, however, was highly significant. Military service was especially helpful for the educational achievement of men from poor families. Consider the following data on average number of years of schooling completed (as of age thirty-six) by the six veteran-status by socioeconomic-status subgroups analyzed:

Subgroup 1: Vietnam veterans of high socioeconomic status: 14.24 years.

Subgroup 2: Vietnam veterans of low socioeconomic status: 13.28 years.

Subgroup 3: Non-Vietnam veterans of high socioeconomic status: 14.02 years.

Subgroup 4: Non-Vietnam veterans of low socioeconomic status: 13.30 years.

Subgroup 5: Nonveterans of high socioeconomic status: 14.74 years.

Subgroup 6: Nonveterans of low socioeconomic status: 12.61 years.

These data show that socioeconomic status had a greater impact on educational achievement at age thirty-six than did veteran status. We infer this from the fact that the difference in the number of years of schooling completed by the richer men (subgroups 1, 3, and 5) versus the poorer men (subgroups 2, 4, and 6) is much larger than the difference between the number of years of schooling completed by the veterans (subgroups 1, 2, 3, and 4) versus the men who never served (subgroups 5 and 6). That point was already made. What about the point at hand regarding the significant interaction of veteran status and socioeconomic status? Veterans of low socioeconomic status (subgroups 2 and 4) had approximately half a year more schooling by age thirty-six than similar nonveterans (subgroup 6). In contrast, veterans of high socioeconomic status (subgroups 1 and 3) had approximately half a year less education than similar nonveterans (subgroup 5). We conclude that military service facilitates the educational development of poor men more than the rich.

This is not surprising in the light of the free-schooling benefits attached to military service in the Vietnam era by the GI bill. The GI bill was enacted by Congress to provide educational or vocational opportunities to veterans whose educational plans were possibly impeded by military service. All individuals who completed a minimum of eighteen months active duty prior to the official end of the Vietnam era were eligible for up to forty-five months of full-time schooling or on-the-job training (Veterans Administration, March 1980). The GI bill was a boon to men from relatively poor families who might not otherwise have had the personal financial resources to pursue a post–high-school education. Our results show that these men took advantage of these educational opportunities.

Military Experiences and Educational Attainment

Service Exit and Return to School

Approximately 23 percent of the Vietnam veterans and 26 percent of the non-Vietnam veterans returned to school and received some educational degree in the year of exit from the service and in the four subsequent years. These percentages are not significantly different from each other, implying that Vietnam veterans and non-Vietnam veterans took immediate advantage of the GI bill to about the same degree.

The issue of when (relative to service exit) the GI bill is used is important because although veterans remain eligible to use the bill for a period of up to ten years following service exit, there appear to be both educational and occupational benefits to using the bill early (Rothbart et al. 1981). Approximately 70 percent of veterans return to school at some point after reentering civilian life, according to Rothbart and colleagues. Yet our data show that only a quarter of veterans have completed a degree in the four years following service exit. A majority of veterans either do not return to school right away, begin school right away but drop out before they have obtained a degree, or begin right away but mix schooling with work so that it takes them longer than four years to get a degree.

All of these factors are probably at work. Rothbart and colleagues found that fewer than 50 percent of veterans resume educational training during the first year following service exit; the earlier the return to school following service exit, the longer the ultimate duration of the educational training period; and the earlier the return to school, the less likely the veteran is to try to work full time while in school. They conclude "Those who did not return early on are likely to show quite diminished achievement, a phenomenon we attribute[d] to the various forces that make effective attendance more difficult as the veteran's return to school is delayed" (p. 302). They go on to speculate:

> Why do some veterans return late? First of all, we have suggested that they are unsettled in the homecoming years (especially Vietnam veterans). Secondly, they may come out without educational plans (which were strongly related to early return) and the decision to return takes time to mature. But additionally, it seems likely that, for some veterans, the decision to return is a consequence of events occurring in the post-military period. Their experience in the labor market may demonstrate the importance of school. Their friends, both veterans and nonveterans, who graduate from college will find relatively better jobs. The strong wage gains of veterans in the early postmilitary years may begin to taper off, and thus, the impulse to make a "human capital" investment may become stronger. Yet, unfortunately, the die that affects the outcome has, to some extent, been cast. The veteran who is late in returning to school is less likely to attend full-time and more likely to have a work career that seriously interferes with his education. One might point out that our argument seems internally contradictory, however. If the veteran has grown less fond of his work career, why does it interfere with school? It would seem logical that, under these circumstances, he ought to make a new start and a strong commitment. But workers ...appear to be conservative. They most often find it necessary to remain at familiar jobs at which they have accumulated tenure." [Pp. 302-303]

It is likely not just the need for remaining in a familiar setting that keeps veterans in the workplace while attending school. The longer they postpone going back to school, the more likely that while in school they will have a family to house, clothe, and feed and that they will need more income than that provided by the GI bill.

The general lesson to be learned from all of this is that if at all possible, early, full-time (or close to full-time) return to school on the part of veterans should be encouraged.

Service-Related Motivations and Behavior and Subsequent Educational Attainment

Tables 3-3 through 3-9 present results from seven statistical analyses of covariance conducted to examine whether certain service-related motivations and behaviors are related to veterans' subsequent educational achievement. In each analysis, the number of years of schooling completed by age thirty-six was the dependent variable. The service-related independent variables hypothesized to be related to eventual educational attainment varied from one analysis to the next. They were:

Mode of service entry (table 3-3).

Military-service branch (table 3-4).

Date of initial military service (table 3-5).

Liquor consumption during service (table 3-6).

Drug use during service (table 3-7).

Disciplinary action during service (table 3-8).

Use of the GI bill after exit from service (table 3-9).

Columns 2 and 3 of each table show that the average academic aptitude and socioeconomic status scores of men in the various subgroups studied were different, often significantly different. (To illustrate, the standard deviations for the academic aptitude and socioeconomic scores were 110 and 10, respectively. Table 3-3 shows that the men who served willingly in the Vietnam era were neither as bright nor as rich as the men who served unwillingly. The academic aptitude differences, especially, were large—close to a full standard deviation.) Because academic aptitude and socioeconomic status are strongly related to subsequent educational attainment, it is important to control for these variables when analyzing the relation between the service-related characteristics of interest and educational attainment. Otherwise we may be documenting differences attributable to academic aptitude or socioeconomic status and not to the service-related characteristic. In our analyses, we have done precisely this. The last two columns of tables 3-3 through 3-9 present each subgroup's average number of

Table 3-3
Relationship between Mode of Service Entry and Years of Education Received by 1981

Modes of Service Entry	Average Academic Aptitude Score	Average Socioeconomic Status Score	Average Number of Years of Education	
			Before Adjusting[a]	After Adjusting[b]**
Drafted, willing	401	95	13.54	13.75
Drafted, unwilling	483	98	14.33	13.87
Enlisted, willing	404	95	13.25	13.45
Enlisted, unwilling	502	98	14.61	14.02
Other	508	101	15.25	14.52

[a]Before adjusting for Vietnam-veteran status, academic aptitude, and socioeconomic status.
[b]After adjusting for Vietnam-veteran status, academic aptitude, and socioeconomic status.
**The difference in years of education among veterans with different modes of service entry was significant at the 0.01 level.

Table 3–4
Relationship between Military-Service Branch and Years of Education Received by 1981

Military-Service Branch	Average Academic Aptitude Score	Average Socioeconomic Status Score	Average Number of Years of Education	
			Before Adjusting[a]	After Adjusting[b]*
Army	425	95	13.82	13.87
Navy	434	98	13.52	13.39
Air Force	457	96	13.95	13.68
Marines	379	94	12.91	13.20

[a]Before adjusting for Vietnam-veteran status, academic aptitude, and socioeconomic status.
[b]After adjusting for Vietnam-veteran status, academic aptitude, and socioeconomic status.
*The difference in years of education among veterans from different branches of military service was significant at the 0.05 level.

Table 3–5
Relationship between Date of Initial Military Service and Years of Education Received by 1981

Date of Initial Military Service	Average Academic Aptitude Score	Average Socioeconomic Status Score	Average Number of Years of Education	
			Before Adjusting[a]	After Adjusting[b]***
Before 1964	383	94	12.51	12.83
1964 or 1965	416	95	13.19	13.28
1966 or later	463	98	14.81	14.55

[a]Before adjusting for Vietnam-veteran status, academic aptitude, and socioeconomic status.
[b]After adjusting for Vietnam-veteran status, academic aptitude, and socioeconomic status.
***The difference in years of education among veterans with different dates of initial military service was significant at the 0.001 level.

years of schooling completed by age thirty-six, both before and after adjusting for veteran status (whether the man served inside or outside the Vietnam-war zone), academic aptitude, and socioeconomic status. The before-adjustment column gives the actual average number of years of schooling completed by men in the subgroup, as of age thirty-six. The after-adjustment column tells what the subgroup's educational attainment would have been if all of the subgroups in the table had had the same veteran status, academic aptitude, and socioeconomic status. The last column thus reflects purer estimates of educational differences attributable to the service-related characteristic of interest. The tables show:

Table 3–6
Relationship between Liquor Consumption during Service and Years of Education Received by 1981

Liquor Consumed during Service	Average Academic Aptitude Score	Average Socioeconomic Status Score	Average Number of Years of Education	
			Before Adjusting[a]	After Adjusting[b]**
Never	434	96	14.20	14.15
Rarely	434	96	13.88	13.85
At least once a month	424	96	13.54	13.56

[a]Before adjusting for Vietnam-veteran status, academic aptitude, and socioeconomic status.
[b]After adjusting for Vietnam-veteran status, academic aptitude, and socioeconomic status.
**The difference in years of education among veterans with different rates of liquor consumption during military service was significant at the 0.01 level.

Table 3–7
Relationship between Drug Use during Service and Years of Education Received by 1981

Drug Use during Service	Average Academic Aptitude Score	Average Socioeconomic Status Score	Average Number of Years of Education	
			Before Adjusting[a]	After Adjusting[b]*
Never	425	96	13.61	13.63
Rarely	433	97	13.88	13.80
At least once a month	439	97	14.56	14.45

[a]Before adjusting for Vietnam-veteran status, academic aptitude, and socioeconomic status.
[b]After adjusting for Vietnam-veteran status, academic aptitude, and socioeconomic status.
*This difference in years of education among veterans with different frequencies of drug use during military service was significant at the 0.05 level.

1. Mode of service entry was significantly related to subsequent educational attainment, with those who served willingly, and especially those who enlisted willingly, having relatively lower educational attainment by age thirty-six than those who served unwillingly (table 3–3).

2. Military-service branch was significantly related to subsequent educational attainment, with service in the army, followed by service in the air force most highly associated with subsequent educational achievement (table 3–4).

3. The earlier the date of initial military service, the lower the eventual educational attainment, probably because the men who joined early were younger at the time of entry and had therefore completed fewer years of education

Table 3-8

Relationship between Disciplinary Action during Service and Years of Education Received by 1981

Disciplinary Action during Service	Average Academic Aptitude Score	Average Socioeconomic Status Score	Average Number of Years of Education	
			Before Adjusting[a]	After Adjusting[b]*
Never	432	96	13.80	13.76
At least once	401	96	13.08	13.30

[a]Before adjusting for Vietnam-veteran status, academic aptitude, and socioeconomic status.
[b]After adjusting for Vietnam-veteran status, academic aptitude, and socioeconomic status.
*The difference in years of education among veterans with and without disciplinary action during service was significant at the 0.05 level.

Table 3-9

Relationship between Use of GI Bill after Service Exit and Years of Education Received by 1981

Use of GI Bill after Service Exit	Average Academic Aptitude Score	Average Socioeconomic Status Score	Average Number of Years of Education	
			Before Adjusting[a]	After Adjusting[b]***
Yes	449	97	14.60	14.42
No	406	95	12.87	13.03

[a]Before adjusting for Vietnam-veteran status, academic aptitude, and socioeconomic status.
[b]After adjusting for Vietnam-veteran status, academic aptitude, and socioeconomic status.
***The difference in years of education among veterans who had and had not used the GI bill after exit from military service was significant at the 0.001 level.

at the time of entry. For these men, the normal on-time course of educational progress was interrupted earlier and with graver consequences (table 3-5).

4. The more liquor consumed during the period of military service, the lower the subsequent educational attainment (table 3-6).

5. Conversely, the greater the amount of admitted drug consumption during the period of military service, the higher the subsequent educational attainment (table 3-7).

6. Having undergone disciplinary action during the service (such as having been demoted or put in the stockade) was associated with lower subsequent educational attainment (table 3-8).

7. Use of the GI bill and its free-schooling provisions subsequent to leaving the military was associated with higher educational attainment—around one and a half years more—as of age thirty-six (table 3-9).

These service-related behaviors are more under an individual's control than the sociodemographic and cognitive characteristics of race, academic ability, and socioeconomic status. Their relation to subsequent educational attainment is thus important to understand and document: men entering the service or considering such entry should realize the potential consequences of their actions. Of course, the findings are correlational in nature: all of the service-related variables examined are correlated or statistically associated with subsequent educational attainment, and we have shown that the relationships documented are not attributable to preservice (socioeconomic status or academic ability) characteristics associated with both the service-related independent variables and the education dependent variable.

It remains to explain the pattern behind the statistical relationships found, to infer more-general conclusions and insights that go beyond the information provided directly by the men. A mixed, multidimensional picture emerges. On the one hand, disciplined behavior within the bounds of good soldiering—little or no liquor consumption, never having been officially disciplined while in the service—is associated with higher subsequent educational attainment. But indicators of active involvement with the surrounding environment, occasionally going beyond the confines of standard conventions and rules—service perceived even a decade after the war as unwilling, some drug usage while in the service, use of the earned benefits of the GI bill following service exit—are also positively related with subsequent educational attainment. Chapter 2 showed that behaviors indicative of active participation in the high-school environment were correlated with subsequent escape from service in an unpopular war. The findings presented in this chapter are consistent with this theme, seemingly pointing to the conclusion that a sense of efficacy spelled the difference between those who benefited educationally from military service and those who did not. The soldier who better knew what he wanted and then went out to get it was able to profit from the military experience.

4

Work and Achievement

The primary question regarding work is whether the interruptions caused by military service are only temporary setbacks from which veterans eventually recover, perhaps even to surpass their matched peers, or whether these interruptions result in more-permanent occupational deficits. We will attempt to answer this question, first, by describing jobs held in 1974 and 1981 (when the men were twenty-nine and thirty-six years old, respectively) in terms of income and job prestige, and second, by examining the men's employment and unemployment histories and relating these to periods of military service. Subgroup differences in the career-related advantages and disadvantages of military service will then be examined in detail to find out for whom and under what circumstances military service is helpful or harmful.

All of the data presented in this chapter are for groups of Vietnam veterans, non-Vietnam veterans, and nonveterans matched on preservice characteristics. Data from the latter two groups therefore will not necessarily correspond to other studies' data from national populations of non-Vietnam veterans and nonveterans.

Occupational Status in 1974

Tables 4-1 through 4-3 present occupation-related data for the three matched groups of men when they were twenty-nine years of age, seven years or so after most of the veterans from the class of 1963 returned from the military to civilian life. The data were obtained from the men's responses to the 1974 Project TALENT survey, conducted several years before the present one was conceived. Various occupational characteristics are described in these tables. Table 4-1 gives some facts about the jobs the men had in 1974; table 4-2 lists the job's characteristics that they reported to be most important to their job satisfaction at that point in their lives; and table 4-3 gives the career goals they saw as being most important for the 1980s, when they would be in their thirties.

Jobs Held

In 1974, men in the three groups were holding different types of jobs (table 4-1). A greater proportion of the two groups of veterans were in jobs in business

Table 4-1
Occupation-Related Characteristics, 1974

Occupation-Related Characteristics	Average, Total Class	Any Significant Difference among Three Matched Groups?	Direction and Magnitude of Significant Difference		
			Average, Vietnam Veterans	Average, Non-Vietnam Veterans	Average, Nonveterans
Career group corresponding to current job (percent)		Yes*			
Engineering, physical science, math, architecture	3.9		1.7	3.4	6.8
Medical and biological sciences	2.0		1.2	2.3	2.2
Business administration	17.1		18.6	18.9	13.6
General teaching and social service	4.8		4.1	3.3	7.3
Humanities, law, social sciences	2.5		2.6	1.9	3.2
Fine arts, performing arts	0.9		0.9	0.5	1.4
Technical jobs	6.0		8.0	6.4	3.5
Proprietors, sales	12.4		11.1	12.9	13.0
Mechanics, industrial trades	13.5		15.2	14.9	10.1
Construction trades	9.5		10.5	8.0	10.3
Secretarial-clerical, office workers	3.6		5.1	3.2	2.6
General labor, public service	23.8		21.1	24.1	26.0
Hourly pay, working men	$4.54	Yes*	$4.40	$4.38	$4.86
Annual pay, working men	$12,642	Yes**	$12,423	$12,040	$13,620
Number of weeks unemployed in past year	0.75	No			
Job satisfaction (percent satisfied)	80	No			

*Significant at 0.05 level.
**Significant at 0.01 level.

administration, in technical jobs, and in jobs in mechanics and the industrial trades. A greater proportion of nonveterans were in engineering, physical science, mathematics, and architecture; in general teaching and social service; and in general labor and public service. Nonveterans tended to have jobs that were draft exempt (teaching, civil service) and jobs requiring a college education, in keeping with the fact that more of them had four-year college degrees. In contrast, veterans had jobs in business and in technical, mechanical, and industrial trades, jobs that tend to require postsecondary vocational training. This is consistent with educational patterns reported previously: significantly more veterans than nonveterans obtain vocational-training licenses.

In part because they were holding different types of jobs, veterans' and nonveterans' incomes at this time were significantly different. On the average, veterans were earning around forty-five cents per hour less than nonveterans. In terms of average annual income, veterans trailed by about $1,400 per year.

In the year prior to the 1974 survey, there were no significant differences in the men's unemployment experiences. However, 1973-1974 was an atypical year; when unemployment patterns reported in the 1981 survey are examined over the twenty-year period 1961 through 1981, greater unemployment is indeed found for veterans.

Finally, table 4-1 shows that at age twenty-nine, there were no significant differences among the three groups of men in job satisfaction. About 80 percent of each group reported that they were satisfied with their jobs.

Characteristics Affecting Job Satisfaction

Table 4-2 lists twenty-five characteristics that prior research has found to be components of job satisfaction. The men in our study were asked to rate each characteristic in terms of how important it was in determining their own job satisfaction. A five-point scale was used, with a 0 standing for "not important at all to my job satisfaction" and a 4 standing for "extremely important to my job satisfaction." In the table, the twenty-five characteristics are listed in order from most important to least important.

The job characteristics rated as being most important to job satisfaction at age twenty-nine were "work that I feel I do well," "work that is challenging and permits me to use my abilities fully," and "interesting work." These character-istics were equally important to veterans and nonveterans.

In general, nonveterans gave higher importance ratings to the set of factors than did veterans; that is, nonveterans were somewhat more demanding of their jobs. They placed significantly greater importance on comfort-related aspects of jobs—good starting salary, short hours, easy work—while simultaneously placing greater importance on aspects of jobs denoting power or independence—freedom to make own decisions and intense, exciting work. This finding may reflect

Table 4-2
Job Characteristics Affecting Satisfaction, 1974

Characteristics Affecting Job Satisfaction	Average Score, Total Class[a]	Any Significant Difference among Three Matched Groups?	Direction and Magnitude of Significant Difference		
			Average, Vietnam Veterans[a]	Average, Non-Vietnam Veterans[a]	Average, Nonveterans[a]
Work that I feel I do well	3.61	No			
Work that is challenging and permits me to use my abilities fully	3.55	No			
Interesting work	3.50	No			
Job security and permanence	3.43	No			
Work that strikes me as important or worthwhile	3.42	No			
Good income expected within a few years	3.41	No			
Opportunity for promotion and advancement	3.37	No			
Freedom to make my own decisions	3.36	Yes**	3.27	3.34	3.48
A supervisor who is competent	3.31	No			
Friendly, likable coworkers	3.10	No			
A supervisor who is pleasant and interested in my welfare	3.07	No			

Work in the area in which I specialized or prepared	2.99	No			
Working in pleasant surroundings	2.98	No			
Good income to start	2.92	Yes*	2.87	2.87	3.02
A job where I know exactly what I am supposed to do	2.88	No			
A job free from racial or sexual bias	2.80	No			
Intense, exciting work	2.75	Yes**	2.74	2.62	2.90
Convenient travel to and from work	2.61	No			
Flexible hours	2.41	No			
A job that gives me status and makes people look up to me	2.17	No			
A job free from pressure and deadlines	2.00	No			
Long vacations	1.98	No			
A job that provides real power	1.59	Yes*	1.60	1.48	1.73
Work that I find easy	1.53	Yes***	1.54	1.33	1.77
Short hours	1.52	Yes*	1.49	1.44	1.66

a 0 = not important; 4 = extremely important.

*Significant at 0.05 level.

**Signfiicant at 0.01 level.

***Significant at 0.001 level.

differences in the characteristics of jobs actually held by veterans and non-veterans. It may also derive from the fact that the veterans had just come home from a military situation providing neither comfortable surroundings nor the opportunity to exercise power (if they were enlisted men, as most of the veterans were). As a consequence, they were not as demanding of their jobs as were nonveterans.

Career Goals

Table 4-3 presents fifteen career goals listed in the order of their rated importance. By far the most-important goal was to "increase my income." This was followed by other goals related to career advancement: "advance or be promoted," "build a good professional reputation," "get further education or training," and "improve my job performance."

In general, veterans placed greater importance on these career goals than nonveterans did. Table 4-2 showed that veterans were not so demanding as nonveterans in terms of job characteristics needed to give them satisfaction. Table 4-3 shows that although veterans came home with fewer demands, they were determined to succeed in their civilian careers. For four of the five career goals rated most important in table 4-3 (all except increasing income), a significantly greater proportion of veterans than matched nonveterans rated each as being important to achieve in the next ten years. One cannot say that the veterans from the class of 1963 came home unmotivated or that their occupational deficits were attributable to any lack of ambition on their part.

Occupational Status in 1981

By 1981, the men in the survey were about thirty-six years old; it had been some ten to fifteen years since most of the veterans returned from the military to civilian life. Table 4-4 presents data on the men's economic status at this point, and table 4-5 presents data on their work-related problems. These tables show that the veterans' 1974 job-related deficits were still present in 1981.

Jobs Held

The first part of table 4-4 gives the occupational distribution of the men in 1981, which is not very different from that of 1974 (table 4-1). There is, however, a moderate amount of individual shifting across career groups that shows up when we analyze data from the two time periods on a case-by-case basis, with forty-one percent of Vietnam veterans, forty percent of non-Vietnam veterans,

Table 4-3
Career Goals, 1974

Most Important Career Goals for Next Ten Years	Percent of Total Class Marking Goal as Important	Any Significant Difference among Three Matched Groups?	Direction and Magnitude of Significant Difference		
			Percent Vietnam Veterans[a]	Percent Non-Vietnam Veterans[a]	Percent Nonveterans[a]
Increase my income	69.8	No			
Advance or be promoted	48.2	Yes*	53.9	45.8	45.2
Build a good professional reputation	44.0	Yes*	48.2	45.2	38.3
Get further education or training	44.0	Yes**	50.1	44.7	36.9
Improve my job performance	39.3	Yes*	43.6	40.2	33.8
Take on more responsibility	36.2	No			
Improve my job security	31.3	No			
Make a contribution to the welfare of others	29.9	No			
Make my job more enjoyable	29.1	No			
Build up my own business	24.5	No			
Work fewer hours than I'm working now	16.8	No			
Get a job in a different field	11.5	No			
Get a job with a different employer in the same field	8.2	No			
Miscellaneous, other	5.6	No			
Work more hours than I'm working now	4.1	No			

[a]Percentage of each group marking goal as important.

*Significant at 0.05 level.

**Significant at 0.01 level.

Table 4-4
Economic Status, 1981

Economic Status Variable	Average, Total Class	Any Significant Difference among Three Matched Groups?	Direction and Magnitude of Significant Difference		
			Average, Vietnam Veterans	Average, Non-Vietnam Veterans	Average, Nonveterans
Occupation-related characteristics					
Career group corresponding to current job (percent)		Yes**			
Engineering, physical science, math, architecture	4.1		1.3	2.9	8.7
Medical and biological sciences	1.7		1.1	2.0	2.0
Business administration	20.0		20.8	22.2	16.4
General teaching and social service	4.8		3.0	4.6	6.8
Humanities, law, social sciences	3.2		3.1	2.9	3.6
Fine arts, performing arts	1.6		1.4	1.0	2.4
Technical jobs	4.9		6.2	4.3	4.2
Proprietors, sales	12.8		13.5	15.2	9.0
Mechanics, industrial trades	12.7		13.9	13.4	10.7
Construction trades	8.3		9.2	7.9	7.7
Secretarial-clerical, office workers	2.1		2.8	1.3	2.5
General labor, public service	23.9		23.7	22.4	25.9

Job-prestige score	45.29	Yes*	43.65	45.96	46.14
Hours worked per week	45.41	No			
Hourly pay, working men	$ 11.06	Yes**	$ 10.53	$ 10.67	$ 12.12
Annual pay, working men	$25,698	Yes*	$24,598	$24,890	$27,912
Number of full-time jobs, 1961–1981	4.26	Yes***	4.33	4.64	3.72
Percent with at least one unemployment spell, 1961–1981	37.4	Yes**	38.2	42.0	31.0
Other economic indicators					
Total family income, 1979 (percent over $20,000)	64.2	Yes*	57.1	65.6	69.8
Percent owning own home	79.2	No			
Percent free from credit problems	82.1	No			
Percent always able to pay bills on time	50.8	No			
Percent with more than one month's income in savings or investments	62.4	No			

*Significant at 0.05 level.
**Significant at 0.01 level.
***Significant at 0.001 level.

and thirty-four percent of nonveterans having changed career groups between the ages of twenty-nine and thirty-six.

Group differences in the men's distribution across the career groups were more pronounced in 1981 than in 1974. By 1981, the veterans had established themselves even more firmly in the world of business and industry (career groups: business administration; proprietors, sales; mechanics, industrial trades); the nonveterans continued to dominate the academic, professional, and public-service worlds (career groups: engineering, physical science, mathematics, architecture; general teaching and social service; general labor, public service).

A job-prestige score was assigned to the primary job held by each working respondent in 1981. Job prestige is an indicator of the amount of prestige or status given to those in a given occupation by American society (Hodge, Siegel, and Rossi 1964). Scores on this variable range from 15 (lunch-counter attendant) to 82 (medical doctor). At age thirty-six, Vietnam veterans were holding jobs with slightly lower prestige scores than were non-Vietnam veterans or nonveterans of comparable background and abilities. The average job-prestige scores for the three matched groups were 43.65, 45.96, and 46.14, respectively. Examples of jobs with prestige scores add meaning to these scores: 42, mail carrier; 43, stenographer; 44, fireman; 45, foreman; 46, electronic technician or machinist; 47, laboratory technician, research assistant in a physics laboratory. These examples show that the group differences in prestige, while statistically significant, were not substantially large.

There were no differences among the three groups in the number of hours worked per week. There were, however, significant income differences, and these were greater than the minor differences in job prestige: veterans were earning $1.50 less per hour than nonveterans, or around $3,000 less per year. Veterans also showed greater job instability over the twenty-year period 1961–1981 than did nonveterans. During this period, veterans had held a greater number of civilian jobs than nonveterans, and a greater proportion of veterans had experienced unemployment (looking for work unsuccessfully for at least one month).

In addition, there were some interesting differences in the labor-force experiences and problems of the two veteran groups. Vietnam veterans had slightly lower incomes than matched non-Vietnam veterans and had held fewer jobs during the 1961–1981 period; a smaller proportion of Vietnam veterans had experienced unemployment in the same period. Closer examination revealed that while a smaller proportion of the Vietnam veterans had experienced unemployment, the jobless spells of those who had tended to be long (most over three months and some over a year). In contrast, the non-Vietnam veterans' spells of unemployment tended to be of only one- to three-months' duration. Combining this finding with the fact that the non-Vietnam veterans had held relatively more jobs by age thirty-six suggests that non-Vietnam veterans may have been more willing than their Vietnam-veteran classmates to accept transitory, or short-term, civilian jobs upon leaving the military. Perhaps the Vietnam veterans needed more time to recover from their military experiences and were less willing to put up with transitory jobs during the reentry period.

Other Indicators of Economic Status

Veterans' families had lower gross incomes in 1979 than nonveterans' families (table 4–4). This is not surprising; veterans had lower incomes than nonveterans, and the men in our study were likely the primary breadwinners for their families. Veterans, however, were not found to be significantly worse off with respect to other economic indicators. There were no significant differences among the three matched groups in percentage owning their own home (about 79 percent), percentage free from credit problems (about 82 percent), percentage always able to pay all their bills on time (about 51 percent), and percentage with more than one month's family income in savings or investments other than their home equity (about 62 percent). The GI bill clearly helped veterans become home owners. One-third of all veterans who owned their own homes did so with the help of the GI bill.

Work-Related Problems

Table 4–5 presents seven work-related problems listed in the order of most importance to men in the study: attaining goals set for oneself, present salary, coping with deadlines and time pressures, getting along with supervisors, following company rules and regulations, getting along with other workers, and being late or absent from work. The most frequently reported problem was attaining goals set for oneself; over forty percent of the men found this to be a minor or major work-related problem. The pervasiveness of this problem probably denotes that a certain degree of restlessness is not unusual in men in their thirties: a striving to get ahead, to achieve goals quickly, to meet internal standards of performance. A greater proportion of veterans than nonveterans reported having major work-related problems dealing with attaining goals they had set and minor work-related problems dealing with following company rules and regulations. Vietnam veterans, especially, had more problems than their peers in getting on track in their work and in abiding by rules to stay on track.

Employment Patterns, Ages Sixteen through Thirty-Six

Thus far, we have examined detailed snapshorts of the occupational and economic status of the men in the study, taken in 1974 and 1981, when the men were twenty-nine and thirty-six years old, corresponding to the years when the

Table 4-5
Work-Related Problems, 1981

Work-Related Problem	Percent of Total Class Reporting This		Any Significant Difference among Three Matched Groups?	Direction and Magnitude of Significant Difference					
				Percent Vietnam Veterans		Percent Non-Vietnam Veterans		Percent Nonveterans	
	As a Minor Problem	As a Major Problem		Minor Problem	Major Problem	Minor Problem	Major Problem	Minor Problem	Major Problem
Attaining goals set for self	36.2	4.3	Yes*	33.9	7.3	36.8	3.6	37.9	1.9
Present salary	29.6	6.6	No						
Coping with deadlines and time pressures	19.4	2.0	No						
Getting along with supervisors	10.2	0.7	No						
Following company rules and regulations	8.1	0.1	Yes*	11.9	0.2	5.3	0.0	7.4	0.3
Getting along with other workers	5.9	0.1	No						
Being late or absent from work	4.5	0.5	No						

*Significant at 0.05 level.

men filled out detailed survey questionnaires about their personal and professional lives. But static snapshots cannot give as much information as moving pictures of a person's or group's progress through time. A snapshot of what a man is doing at age thirty-six does not tell how he got to where he is or how long he has been there. Moreover, occasionally snapshots can convey misleading impressions, since economic, political, social, and other environmental conditions sometimes create atypical years that are quite different from normal times.

In the 1981 survey, we therefore asked the men to provide their complete employment and unemployment histories: descriptions of all full-time jobs they had held since they left the ninth grade, along with beginning and ending dates (month and year) for each of these jobs, and also dates of each unemployment spell experienced during this period. To ease the burden on the respondents, we did not ask for income histories. Other studies have shown that people find it difficult, if not impossible, to recall accurately how their income has changed from year to year. For the same reason, we did not ask for information on unemployment periods of less than one month.

Figure 4-1 charts the average job-prestige scores for members of the three groups who were working in the civilian labor force during the 1961-1981 period, which covers their entire working life. Only civilian jobs are reflected in the figure; because of the temporary nature of military assignments, these jobs were excluded from the figure. Figure 4-2 then summarizes the groups' unemployment histories by charting the percentage of men in each group who reported being unemployed at least one month in each of the twenty years.

The Course of Job Prestige

The prestige level of the men's jobs tended to climb rapidly in the initial stages of the work life and then to taper off (figure 4-1). As was the case with the education curves presented in chapter 3 the job-prestige curve for nonveterans rises faster and earlier than the veterans' curves and stabilizes (reaches its peak) earlier. The job-prestige curves for the three groups are very similar until around 1965, when the Vietnam draft began to gain momentum. Job-prestige deficits on the part of working veterans began to emerge about this time. These deficits grew in succeeding years, becoming most pronounced in the 1968-1973 period, when most veterans were returning and readjusting to civilian life. The return period was obviously a trying one for the veterans. The data show without question that military service is a powerful disruptor of the normal course of career development.

How lasting are these negative effects? By 1974, the non-Vietnam veterans were not far behind nonveterans in terms of job prestige, and by 1979, they had completely caught up. (The catching up did not apply to income; non-Vietnam veterans continued to lag behind nonveterans at age thirty-six in income.) In

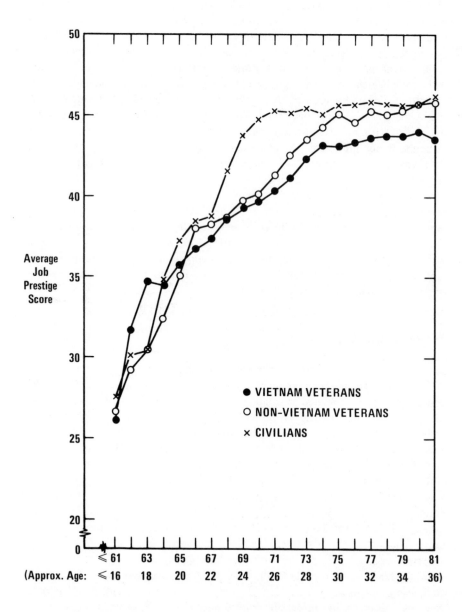

Figure 4-1. Average Prestige Score of Civilian Jobs Held by Three Study Groups, 1961–1981

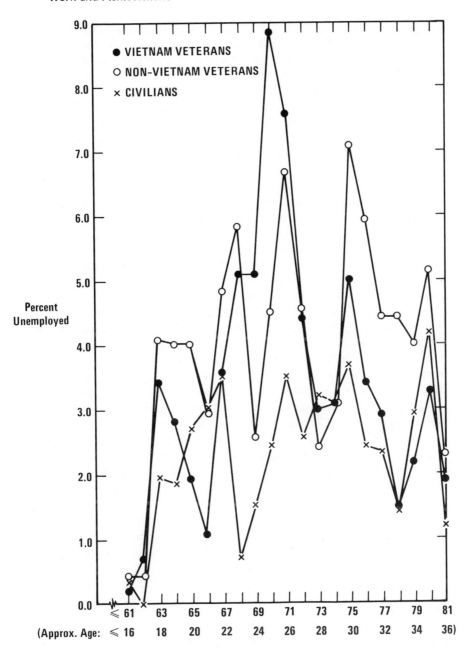

Note: Actual percentages are higher than the ones shown here because 10 percent of the sample reported that they had had at least one unemployment spell but failed to report in what year(s) the spells occurred.

Figure 4-2. Percentage of Each Study Group Reporting Being Unemployed at Least One Month, 1961–1981

contrast, the job-prestige curve for Vietnam veterans gives no evidence that this group will ever catch up with their nonveteran classmates; Vietnam veterans reached their peak job prestige in 1974, and there is no gain after this date. As seen previously, Vietnam veterans' occupational deficits were also found in terms of the income variable.

What are the reasons behind these continuing occupational deficits? Other studies have shown that men's incomes and job prestige tend to rise with job experience or tenure. For men in certain kinds of careers, job shifts or changes are another important vehicle for achieving income and prestige increases. This is in interesting contrast to women's typical career patterns. For women, the shape of the income and prestige curves is flatter throughout the life course. At age fifty, women are generally not earning significantly more money or holding jobs with significantly higher prestige than either other females aged thirty at the time or than they themselves did twenty years prior, when they were thirty. In addition, job shifts for women, are often not associated with furthering their careers, especially when the shift comes after a temporary withdrawal from the labor force (for example, to have and raise children) or after a forced job move (perhaps to a new city where the husband has accepted a higher-paying job) (Suter and Miller 1973; Spilerman 1977; King 1977, Rosenfeld 1978; Card, Steel, and Abeles 1980; Sorensen and Tuma 1981). The veterans, and especially the Vietnam veterans, all of whom are male, do not appear to follow the general male pattern of significant pay and prestige increases with age, tenure, and job shifts. (Despite their absence from the civilian labor force while in the military, veterans had held a significantly greater number of civilian jobs than nonveterans by age thirty-six.) One can speculate that this is because, as is the case for women, many veterans choose careers in the secondary labor market, characterized by good pay to start but little potential for subsequent significant salary increases (for women, secretarial jobs, and for veterans, jobs in the mechanical and industrial trades); veterans' job shifts come after a temporary withdrawal from the civilian labor force: military service, like child rearing, is a career interruption causing human capital to atrophy and from which one therefore needs time to recover; finally, for many women as well as veterans, the job shift may be the result of negative rather than positive forces (for example, for women, a husband's move to a new city to improve his own career prospects, and for veterans, a move instigated by problems on the old job).

The Course of Unemployment

Figure 4-2 charts the three groups' unemployment experiences in the 1961–1981 period by showing the percentage of each group that was unemployed for at least one month in each of the twenty years. The data in this figure are a slight underestimate of true unemployment in the groups because 10 percent of the study sample reported that they had had at least one unemployment spell during this period but failed to report when the spell had occurred. These men's unemployment experiences could not be represented in the graph. This fact does not invalidate the information contained in the graph concerning the relative position of each group in each year because the proportions of men with missing information were equally divided among the three groups.

This figure shows the erratic, cyclical nature of unemployment patterns. In 1970, 1971, 1975, and 1980, unemployment rates for all of the groups were up. In general, unemployment rates for the two veteran groups were higher than corresponding rates for nonveterans. The group differences were largest between 1968 and 1972, the years of the veterans' reentry. Because the data in this and figure 4-1 appear to link the most-severe occupational deficits to this period, the next four graphs pursue the issue in greater detail.

Before we leave figure 4-2, however, we should point out an interesting difference in the unemployment patterns of the two veteran groups. Between 1969 and 1971, immediately following the men's return to civilian life, the unemployment rate for Vietnam veterans was higher than that for non-Vietnam veterans. After 1975, the reverse was true. Apparently Vietnam veterans catch up with non-Vietnam veterans in terms of being gainfully employed; however, as we saw in the previous section they do not catch up correspondingly in terms of income or job prestige.

Unemployment and Job-Prestige Patterns following Service Exit

Figures 4-3 and 4-4 show the unemployment and job-prestige patterns for the two veteran groups in the service-exit year and the four subsequent years. Both figures show a gain in occupational status with the passage of time. For both groups, the trend in unemployment is downward and that for job prestige upward. These gains were consistently more rapid for the non-Vietnam veterans, however. Why did the Vietnam veterans have a more-difficult time than other veterans in overcoming occupation-related problems? We examined two possible explanations: that the Vietnam veterans' slower progress was a result of combat stress and its aftereffects or that it was a function of the different homecoming given by the country to the two veteran groups, with the occupational adjustment of the Vietnam veteran being hampered by the greater antiwar sentiment heaped upon him.

We tested the first hypothesis by examining whether, within the group of Vietnam veterans, those who had experienced no combat or light combat had higher 1974 and 1981 incomes, higher 1981 job prestige, or less-severe unemployment problems during the 1961-1981 period than those who had experienced heavy combat. Consistent with findings from other studies (Penk et al.

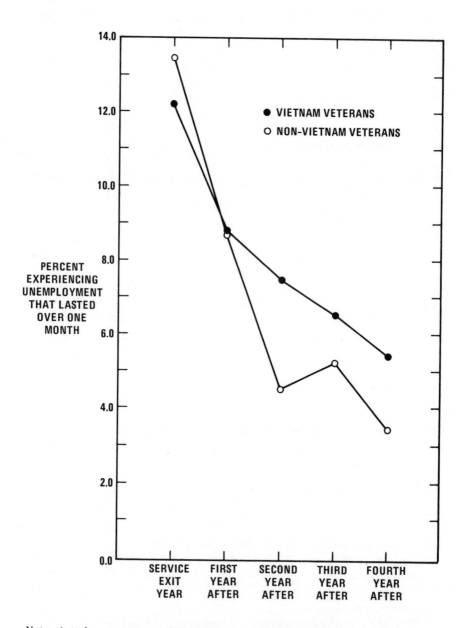

Note: Actual percentages are higher than the ones shown here because 10 percent of
respondents reported that they had had at least one unemployment spell but failed
to report when the spell(s) occurred, and 4 percent of respondents did not report
their service exit year. Data from these individuals are not reflected in the graph.

Figure 4-3. Percentage of Groups of Vietnam Veterans and Non-Vietnam
Veterans Reporting Being Unemployed for at Least One Month in
the Service-Exit and Four Following Years.

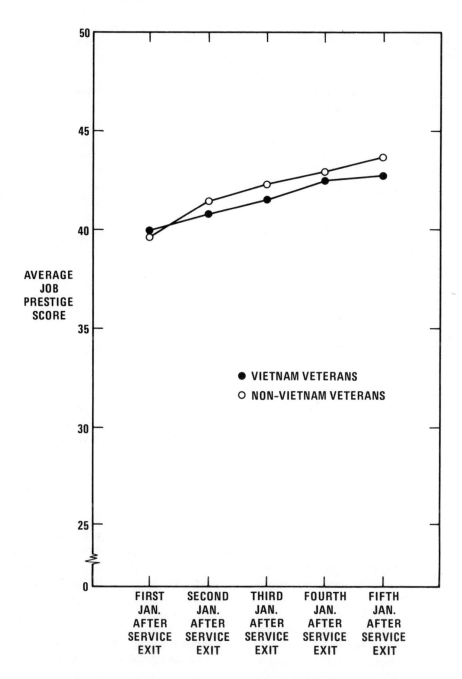

Figure 4-4. Average Prestige Score of Jobs Held by Groups of Vietnam Veterans and Non-Vietnam Veterans in the Five Januaries following Separation from the Military

1981; Rothbart et al. 1981), we found no differences in income, job prestige, or unemployment attributable to the intensity of combat experienced.

We tested the second hypothesis by analyzing unemployment and job-prestige patterns separately for veterans who returned home in different years, because the country's attitude toward the Vietnam conflict became significantly less favorable as that war dragged on into the 1970s. Figures 4–5 and 4–6 show that, in keeping with the second hypothesis, the occupational-status differences between the two veteran groups were largest for the groups of veterans who came home in the post-1970 period, when antiwar sentiment was high. Although the early 1970s were also an era of hard economic times in the country, both veteran groups had to face the identical economic situation upon their return home. Economic reasons therefore cannot explain the findings. Rather, the data are consistent with the hypothesis that the political climate did make a difference, but our survey cannot tell us why. Perhaps Vietnam veterans were discriminated against in the job market; perhaps the country's antiwar feelings alienated them and made them withdraw from coping wholeheartedly with re-entry problems.

Group Differences in Occupational Returns to the Education Investment

Veterans and nonveterans did not differ in terms of the average number of years of schooling they had completed by age thirty-six; however, they did differ in terms of when and where this schooling was obtained, with nonveterans tending to complete their schooling earlier and tending to obtain college, as opposed to vocational noncollege, degrees. There were significantly greater occupational deficits on the part of veterans relative to what might be expected on the basis of their educational accomplishments. Veterans had significantly greater unemployment rates than nonveterans. In addition, working veterans had jobs associated with lower prestige and income than nonveterans.

These findings, considered together, imply that veterans are not as able as nonveterans to translate their educational achievement into occupational achievement. The data in table 4–6 show that this is so. The left half of the table gives the correlation, or degree of association, between number of years of schooling and job-prestige score, hourly pay, and yearly pay for the three groups. The correlations for nonveterans (in the last row) are all higher than the corresponding correlations for veterans. The right half of the table shows the effect of one additional year of schooling on the groups' job prestige and income. On the average, each additional year of schooling adds 3.54 points to nonveterans' job prestige but only 2.31 points to Vietnam veterans' job prestige and 3.12 points to non-Vietnam veterans' job prestige. The same additional year of schooling adds ninety-seven cents per hour ($2,190 per year) to nonveterans' pay, but

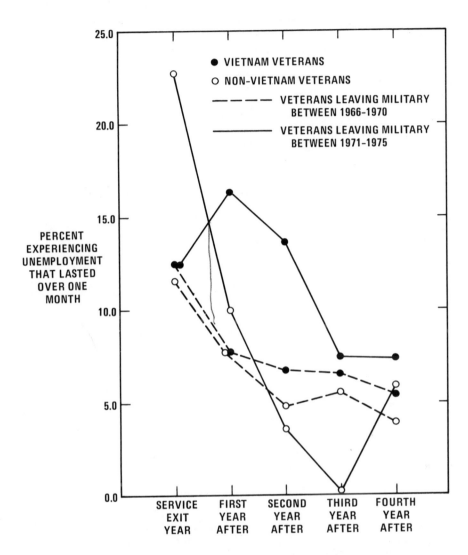

Note: Actual percentages are higher than the ones shown here because 10 percent of respondents reported that they had had at least one unemployment spell but failed to
report when the spell(s) occurred, and 4 percent of respondents did not report their
service exit year. Data from these individuals are not reflected in the graph.

Data for veterans leaving the military between 1961 and 1965 are not included because of unreliability owing to the small sample sizes involved.

Figure 4-5. Percentage of Groups of Vietnam Veterans and Non-Vietnam
Veterans Reporting Being Unemployed for at Least One Month in
the Service-Exit and Four Following Years, by Service-Exit Period.

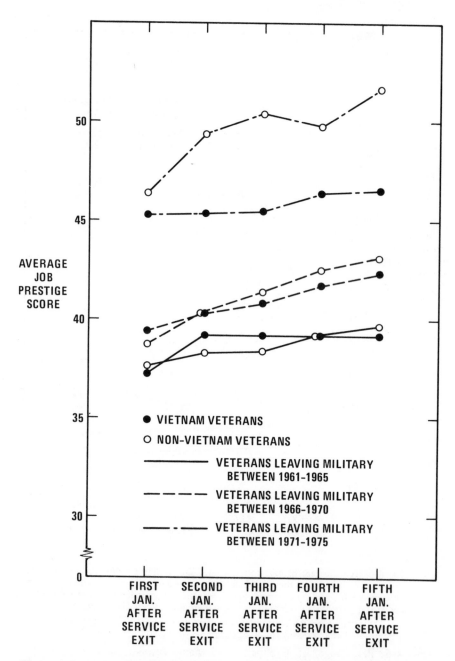

Figure 4-6. Average Prestige Score of Jobs Held by Groups of Vietnam Veterans and Non-Vietnam Veterans in the Five Januaries following Separation from the Military, by Service-Exit Period

Table 4-6
Impact of Education on Job Prestige and Income at Age Thirty-Six

Group	Correlation with Number of Years of Schooling			Effect of One Additional Year of Schooling		
	Job-Prestige Score	Hourly Pay	Yearly Pay	On Job-Prestige Score	On Hourly Pay	On Yearly Pay
Vietnam veterans	0.43***	0.20***	0.20***	+2.31 points	+66c	+$1,598
Non-Vietnam veterans	0.54***	0.15***	0.16***	+3.12 points	+34c	+$ 906
Nonveterans	0.65***	0.29***	0.25***	+3.54 points	+97c	+$2,190

***Significant at 0.001 level.

only sixty-six cents per hour ($1,598 per year) to Vietnam veterans' pay and thirty-four cents per hour ($906 per year) to non-Vietnam veterans' pay.

Why are the occupation-related returns to the education investment lower for veterans than for nonveterans? We examined six possible explanations for this puzzling finding:

1. Veterans get different kinds of post-high-school degrees than do nonveterans, with the former tending to get vocational-training licenses and the latter college degrees. College degrees have relatively higher payoff in terms of future job prestige and income because they lead to jobs in the primary (as opposed to secondary) labor market sector where career lines with clear advancement pathways are found.
2. Veterans finish schooling later than nonveterans. Our study did not give veterans' education sufficient time to pay off, because our latest data collection took place when the men were only thirty-six.
3. Nonveterans have acquired greater seniority on their civilian jobs, in part because they finished schooling earlier but also because veterans change jobs more frequently.
4. Some veterans left the military when the economic situation in the United States was unfavorable and the country's antiwar sentiment was at a peak. These environmental conditions made it difficult for these veterans to adjust to civilian life.
5. Veterans have more-severe psychological problems than nonveterans, (as the next chapter will show), and these problems keep them from getting ahead.
6. Some veterans have had combat experience whose aftereffects hamper their occupational adjustment in a civilian setting.

To test these hypotheses, we created the following variables from information provided by veterans and nonveterans in the 1981 survey:

1. *Vocational Degree,* scored as 0 or 1, depending on whether the respondent got a vocational degree after high school.
2. *Year Finish School,* defined as the year the respondent completed his last (highest) degree.
3. *Job Seniority,* defined as the starting date of the respondent's current job for respondents who were employed when the 1981 survey was conducted.
4. *Military Exit,* scored as 0 or 1, depending on whether the respondent left the military during the problematic years (1971–1975). (This score was automatically set to 0 for nonveterans.)
5. *Problems,* defined as the respondent's total score on three psychological scales measuring anxiety, hostility, and depression.
6. *Combat,* defined as the respondent's score on a scale measuring the intensity of combat experienced while in the military. (The score on the scale was automatically set to 0 for non-Vietnam veterans and for nonveterans.)

For the most part, veterans and nonveterans did differ on these characteristics (table 4–7):

1. Twice as many veterans as nonveterans had vocational degrees by the age of thirty-six.
2. On the average, veterans finished school about a year later than nonveterans.
3. Contrary to expectations, there were no significant differences between veterans and nonveterans in seniority on their current jobs. Both groups had been on these current jobs some seven to eight years, on the average.
4. Exit date from the military was not applicable to the nonveteran group. Comparable proportions of Vietnam veterans and non-Vietnam veterans (11 percent and 12 percent, respectively) had left the military in the post-1970 antiwar period.
5. Vietnam veterans had greater psychological problems than non-Vietnam veterans or nonveterans, as indicated by a significantly higher average score on the combined anxiety, hostility, and depression scale.
6. The combat scale was applicable only to Vietnam veterans. All men in the other two groups were assigned a zero score on this scale, automatically giving them a different profile from Vietnam veterans on this variable.

Contrary to our expectations, however, not one of the six characteristics was strongly associated with job prestige or income. For this reason, taking the six explanatory variables into account (in statistical regressions of job prestige and income) did not eliminate or even reduce the significant group differences in the prestige and income returns to the educational investment.

Table 4-7
Means and Correlations Associated with Hypothesized Explanatory Variables

Hypothesized Explanatory Variable	Average Score			Are These Group Differences Significant?	Correlation with Job Prestige		Correlation with Annual Income	
	Vietnam Veterans	Non-Vietnam Veterans	Nonveterans		Before Adjusting for Education	After Adjusting for Education	Before Adjusting for Education	After Adjusting for Education
Vocational degree	0.23	0.22	0.11	Yes***	-0.07	0.05	-0.07	-0.03
Year finish school	68.8	68.1	67.4	Yes**	0.34	0.05	0.06	-0.08
Job seniority	72.7	73.4	72.8	No	0.14	0.01	0.05	-0.00
Military exit	0.11	0.12	0.0	Yes***	0.08	-0.02	0.04	0.00
Problems	21.75	20.55	20.85	Yes***	-0.17	-0.10	-0.08	-0.05
Combat	21.60	0.0	0.0	Yes***	-0.12	-0.11	-0.06	-0.05

**Significant at 0.01 level.
***Significant at 0.001 level.

We conclude, therefore, that nonveterans are able to get more occupational returns (higher job prestige and income) for their educational investments than veterans are. Why this is so cannot be established from the data collected for this study. Did a significant proportion of veterans just linger in school to get their GI bill benefits, without clear goals while in school or after school? Were veterans indeed discriminated against in the job market in the aftermath of the war? Did veterans negotiate less forcefully for their jobs and their incomes? (Recall that in 1960, at age fifteen, nonveterans scored higher than veterans on behavioral and attitudinal indicators of control and efficacy, and in 1974, at age twenty-nine, nonveterans were more demanding than veterans in terms of aspects of jobs that would give them satisfaction.) These speculations cannot directly be proved or disproved with our data, but they should be considered plausible explanations for our occupation-related findings.

Subgroup Differences in the Occupational Consequences of Military Service

We now look into whether the occupational consequences of military service are different for men coming from different family backgrounds, for men with different academic abilities, or for men differing in why they entered the military and how they conducted themselves while in the service.

Income Differences at Age Thirty-Six for Men from Different Backgrounds

Three statistical analyses of covariance were conducted to investigate to what extent differences in the men's annual income at age thirty-six were attributable to their veteran status, race, academic abilities, socioeconomic origins, and/or educational attainment. In each analysis, annual income (as reported in the 1981 survey) was treated as the dependent variable. The independent variables, or the variables hypothesized to account for income differences, varied from one analysis to the next. In the first analysis, they were veteran status and race; in the second, veteran status and academic aptitude; in the third, veteran status and the socioeconomic status of the man's parents while he was in the ninth grade. Educational attainment at age thirty-six was treated as a covariate in each analysis. (A covariate is a variable hypothesized to be associated with both the dependent and independent variables. When the covariate is statistically controlled, one can note whether the relationship between the dependent and independent variables persists. If it does, the covariate does not completely account for the relationship; if it does not, the covariate does account for the relationship.)

These analyses yielded answers to three sets of questions:

1. Can income differences at age thirty-six be accounted for by individual differences in veteran status, race, academic abilities, and socioeconomic status?
2. To what extent does the association between income and these independent variables persist when educational level is held constant? That is, to what extent is the association between income and the independent variables explained by the fact that whites, the bright, and the economically well off are better educated than nonwhites, the less bright, and the less well off, and therefore (solely because of this higher education) earn more money?
3. Are there significant interaction effects among the independent variables? That is, are the income advantages and disadvantages of military service equally distributed among whites versus nonwhites, bright men versus less-bright men, and economically well-off versus less-well-off men?

Table 4-8 summarizes the answers to these questions. Veteran status, race, academic aptitude, and socioeconomic status were all significantly associated with income at age thirty-six, with nonveterans, whites, individuals with higher-than-average academic abilities, and individuals from economically advantaged families earning more at this age than veterans, nonwhites, individuals with lower-than-average academic abilities, and individuals from families with lower-than-average socioeconomic status.

All of these significant associations, with the exception of that between academic aptitude and income, remained when educational level was held constant. This means that the primary reason the bright are earning more money than the less bright at midlife is that the former have acquired significantly more years of schooling. The income deficits of veterans, nonwhites, and the economically disadvantaged are not explained completely by their lower educational achievement, however. The previous section has explored some reasons for the income deficits of veterans. Exploration of reasons for the income deficits of nonwhites and the economically disadvantaged lies beyond the scope of this study. Discrimination is one possible explanation; so is the possibility that members of these disadvantaged subgroups do not possess the resources or traits required to get ahead in this society, such as persistence, contacts, mentors, role models, knowledge of how to play the game, and so on.

None of the interactions of veteran status with race, academic aptitude, or socioeconomic status was statistically significant. This means that the negative occupational consequences of military service were equally applicable to whites and nonwhites, individuals of low and high academic ability, and economically advantaged and disadvantaged individuals. The impact of military service on these subgroups' incomes at midlife was of relatively equal magnitude.

Table 4-8
Effect of Veteran Status Group, Race, Academic Aptitude, and
Socioeconomic Status on Annual Income at Age Thirty-Six

Factor Hypothesized to Influence Annual Income	Was Factor Significantly Related to Annual Income?		What Was Nature of Significant Relationship?
	Before Adjusting for Education Level	*After Adjusting for Education Level*	
Main effects			
Veteran status group[a]	Yes*	Yes**	Nonveterans had the highest annual income, followed by non-Vietnam veterans and then by Vietnam veterans
Race[b]	Yes**	Yes**	Nonwhites were earning $4,500 less per year than whites
Academic aptitude[c]	Yes***	No	Those with above-average academic aptitude were earning more than those with below-average academic aptitude; however, the difference disappeared when the higher educational level of the bright men was taken into account
Socioeconomic status[c]	Yes***	Yes*	Those with above-average socioeconomic status were earning more than those with below-average socioeconomic status
Interaction effects			
Group x race	No	No	
Group x academic aptitude	No	No	
Group x socioeconomic status	No	No	

Source: Data obtained from three analyses of covariance, all of which used annual income reported in the 1981 survey as dependent variable. The independent variables in the first ANOVA were veteran status group and race. The independent variables in the second ANOVA were veteran status group and academic aptitude score in 1960. The independent variables in the third ANOVA were veteran status group and parents' socioeconomic status, as reported in 1960. Educational attainment was treated as a covariate in all analyses.

[a]There were three matched veteran status groups: Vietnam veterans, non-Vietnam veterans, and nonveterans.

[b]There were two racial categories: white and nonwhite.

[c]There were two academic aptitude and two socioeconomic status categories: above average (for the class) and below average.

*Significant at the 0.05 level.

**Significant at the 0.01 level.

***Significant at the 0.001 level.

Military Experiences and Subsequent Income

Finally, we investigated the extent to which various experiences prior to, during, and after the period of military service were associated with veterans' income at age thirty-six. We examined the degree of association between income at age thirty-six and seven service-related motivations and behaviors: mode of service entry, military-service branch, date of initial military service, liquor consumption during service, drug use during service, disciplinary action during service, and use of the GI bill after exit from service. All of these variables were significantly related to educational attainment. In our present analyses, we found only three of the variables to be related to income at age thirty-six: mode of service entry, date of initial military service, and disciplinary action during service:

1. Men who were drafted had lower incomes at age thirty-six than men who enlisted (table 4-9).
2. Men who joined the military before 1966 had lower incomes at age thirty-six than men who joined in or after this year (table 4-10).
3. Men who were disciplined formally while in the service had lower incomes at age thirty-six than men who were never disciplined (table 4-11).

Table 4-9
Relationship between Mode of Service Entry and Annual Income at Age Thirty-Six

Modes of Service Entry	Average Annual Income		
	Before Adjusting[a]	After Adjusting for Background Variables[b] **	After Adjusting for Background Variables and Education Level[c] *
Drafted, willing	$21,575	$21,899	$21,837
Drafted, unwilling	23,229	22,574	22,441
Enlisted, willing	23,878	24,206	24,438
Enlisted, unwilling	27,534	26,648	26,411
Other	32,802	31,455	30,732

[a]Before adjusting for Vietnam-veteran status, academic aptitude, socioeconomic status, and education level.

[b]After adjusting for Vietnam-veteran status, academic aptitude, and socioeconomic status.

[c]After adjusting for Vietnam-veteran status, academic aptitude, socioeconomic status, and education level.

*These differences in annual income among veterans with different modes of service entry were significant at the 0.05 level.

**These differences in annual income among veterans with different modes of service entry were significant at the 0.01 level.

Table 4-10

Relationship between Date of Initial Military Service and Annual Income at Age Thirty-Six

	Average Annual Income		
Date of Initial Military Service	Before Adjusting[a]	After Adjusting for Background Variables[b]*	After Adjusting for Background Variables and Education Level[c]
Before 1964	$23,492	$24,212	$24,856
1964 or 1965	22,340	22,611	22,935
1966 or later	26,905	26,242	25,605

[a]Before adjusting for Vietnam-veteran status, academic aptitude, socioeconomic status, and education level.

[b]After adjusting for Vietnam-veteran status, academic aptitude, and socioeconomic status.

[c]After adjusting for Vietnam-veteran status, academic aptitude, socioeconomic status, and education level.

*These differences in annual income among veterans with different modes of service entry were significant at the 0.05 level.

Table 4-11

Relationship between Disciplinary Action during Service and Annual Income at Age Thirty-Six

	Average Annual Income		
Disciplinary Action during Service	Before Adjusting[a]	After Adjusting for Background Variables[b]*	After Adjusting for Background Variables and Education Level[c]*
Never	$25,181	$25,152	$25,096
At least once	20,706	20,901	21,314

[a]Before adjusting for Vietnam-veteran status, academic aptitude, socioeconomic status, and education level.

[b]After adjusting for Vietnam-veteran status, academic aptitude, and socioeconomic status.

[c]After adjusting for Vietnam-veteran status, academic aptitude, socioeconomic status, and education level.

*These differences in annual income among veterans with different modes of service entry were significant at the 0.05 level.

The size of the income differences between these subgroups of men, shown in the first data column of tables 4-9 through 4-11, ranged from $1,500 to over $10,000 per year.

We next explored the possibility that the income differences were due to one or both of the following covariates: preexisting background differences among the subgroups (the fact that men who were drafted, who signed up early for their military stint, and who were disciplined while in the service were neither as bright nor as rich as their classmates), and educational attainment differences among the subgroups (the fact that men with income deficits had lower educational levels than men without income deficits).

The last two columns of tables 4-9 through 4-11 give the subgroups' annual income at age thirty-six when subgroup differences in the background variables are held constant and when subgroup differences in both the background variables and current educational level are held constant. Controlling for the background variables did not eliminate any of the significant differences; the relatively lower incomes of men who were drafted, men who joined the military before 1966, and men who were disciplined while in the service could not be explained completely by their lower academic abilities and socioeconomic status. When education was added to the background variables as a covariate, one of the significant associations—that between date of service entry and income—disappeared. This implies that the reason those who enter the service early have lower incomes a decade or so after their service exit is that early entry into the military is associated with curtailed schooling. In contrast, the income deficits of the drafted and disciplined subgroups persisted even after controlling for their lower educational attainment. This means that these subgroups' lower educational attainment does not completely explain why they were earning less at age thirty-six. We need to look for other reasons for this income deficit—possibly a lack of ability to control the environment or of knowledge of how to play the game. In addition, disciplinary action while in service was likely associated with a less-than-honorable military discharge, a factor adversely affecting future employment and employability. The present study cannot test the validity of these possible explanations. We do have enough information to propose, however, that, as was the case for the educational consequences of military service, it was the men who knew what they wanted and how to stay on track to get it who were able to recover from the damaging interruptions to career development brought about by military service.

Summary

Military service, especially service in the Vietnam fire zone, has resulted in career-related deficits for Vietnam-era veterans: higher unemployment rates, lower job prestige, and lower income relative to their matched ninth-grade classmates who did not serve. The income deficit is found as late as ten to fifteen years after the veterans' reentry into civilian life. It remains when educational and other differences among the groups are controlled. All major subgroups of veterans—whites and nonwhites, economically advantaged and disadvantaged, bright and less bright—are hurt, in relatively equal fashion. Within the veteran groups, the subsequent careers of those drafted into service and/or disciplined during service are especially affected. Careers of veterans who served in the Vietnam fire zone are impeded more severely and in longer-lasting fashion than are careers of veterans who were never assigned to Vietnam. For example, by age thirty-six the latter group has completely caught up with nonveterans in terms of job prestige. Vietnam veterans have not caught up; their job-prestige trend since service exit suggests that they never will. The reason for the continuing occupation-related problems of Vietnam veterans is somewhat unclear; the combat experience alone does not appear to be the explanation.

These findings are consistent with those of other investigators who have studied other groups of Vietnam veterans and their peers in controlled, scientific fashion (for example, Rothbart et al. 1981). They contradict more-sanguine conclusions based on raw income figures obtained from unmatched groups of veterans and nonveterans, for example, the conclusion that Vietnam-era veterans are better off, occupationally, than their age-mates because the former group's incomes are higher ("$12,680 in 1977, compared with $9,820 for non-vets aged 20 to 39") and their unemployment rates lower (by one percentage point in 1978) (statement attributed to VA administrator Max Cleland in *Newsweek*, November 12, 1979, p. 49).

This conclusion is misleading for several reasons. It does not take into account the fact that the two groups being compared were different to begin with, even prior to the military service of the veterans. Military-selection policies exclude the least able from participation. Also, veterans had higher educational attainment than nonveterans—in terms of proportion with a high-school degree—even before they entered service. In addition, the cited samples include men from multiple birth cohorts—all men aged twenty to thirty-nine in 1977. Because income tends to increase with age and seniority, it can be misleading to compare raw income figures for men of different ages unless there is the same proportion of veterans and nonveterans in each age cohort (a condition not met in the present instance). The cited figures lump Vietnam veterans and nonveterans together, another source of imprecision, given the fact taht the occupational consequences of military service are more severe for the former group. Finally, the cited data consist of measurements taken at a single point in time. This chapter has demonstrated that such a procedure can lead to misleading conclusions. Unemployment figures especially tend to be cyclical and erratic. There are atypical years not representative of the general moving picture through time. Rothbart and colleagues (1981) have shown that income figures favoring Vietnam-era veterans over their nonveteran peers actually reverse themselves when statistical controls for the different family and educational backgrounds of the men are introduced. Our data corroborate those of Rothbart and his colleagues, establishing the long-lasting negative consequences of military service in the Vietnam era for men's subsequent civilian careers.

5

Physical, Social, and Psychological Health

Background

The effect of service in Vietnam on soldiers' subsequent physical and (especially) mental health has been the most widely studied aspect of the personal aftermath of the war. Most early studies involved small groups of Vietnam veterans, often help-seeking groups (veterans who came to counselors, clinics, or hospitals for a variety of problems relating to physical health, mental health, and substance abuse). Occasionally control (comparison) groups of non-Vietnam veterans and nonveterans were also studied, but seldom were the control groups matched with the Vietnam-veteran group in terms of preservice characteristics. Information on preservice characteristics, if gathered, was obtained through retrospective self-reports, a method that has been shown to be reliable for certain kinds of information, such as demographic background, but not for others, such as attitudes and other kinds of subjective information. The general finding has been that veterans, especially Vietnam veterans, come back to civilian life with a variety of physical, social, and psychological problems (DeFazio 1975; Helzer Robins, and Davis 1976). However, there has been disagreement on the prevalence, severity, and permanence of these problems. Not surprisingly, studies of help-seeking veterans have documented pervasive and serious problems. Studies utilizing national samples of veterans and comparison groups of nonveterans have also found problems that appear to be attributable to combat, but fewer if any problems that appear to be attributable to the military experience itself.

The literature is divided on the permanence of these postcombat psychological problems. Proponents of the stress-evaporation model, led by Worthington (1977, 1978), claim that these problems are seldom long lasting; when they are, the long-term effects are attributable to adjustment problems that were present before the military stint. Proponents of the residual-stress model, led by Figley (1978a), claim that these problems persist many years after the actual traumatic combat events are experienced. The persistence is an inherent feature of the postcombat disorder labeled posttraumatic stress disorder by the American Psychiatric Association. Data from the recent study commissioned by Congress (volume 3 by Laufer et al. and volume 4 by Kadushin et al. 1981) appear to support the residual-stress model. Laufer, Kadushin, and their colleagues found that during, immediately after, and more than a decade after the Vietnam war, a greater proportion of Vietnam veterans than nonVietnam veterans or nonveterans were stressed. The intensity of combat experienced by Vietnam veterans was significantly associated with the incidence of stress symptoms, with increased anger and hostility, and with increased rates of drinking and arrests. Minority status, low educational attainment, low income, and irregular or unsatisfying employment were also associated with higher levels of stress. These negative association were reduced or eliminated for combat veterans who fought in the early (pre-1968) years of the war, before public support for the conflict disappeared, for combat veterans who received positive social support from their spouse upon return from military service, for combat veterans who came from stable families of origin, for veterans in large cities who had many Vietnam-veteran friends, and for veterans in smaller cities and towns with friends who formed a community, each knowing one another.

Overview of Issues and Procedures

We will address these issues of incidence, severity, and permanence of health-related problems from our unique research-design perspective, compare our findings with those of prior investigations, and evaluate the evidence for and against the hypothesis that combat leads to long-lasting residual stress. All intergroup comparisons will be done with Vietnam veterans, non-Vietnam veterans, and nonveterans matched in terms of fifty-one preservice character-istics. The focus will be limited to long-term consequences of service and combat as measured at a single point in time, age thirty-six. We are unable to give an account of the changing physical and mental health of the men in the decade following their period of military service because we did not ask for health histories in the 1981 survey. Although the work of other investigators has shown that individuals can remember accurately education and work histories, we found no evidence in the literature that people can remember accurately the changing severity of their personal problems. Rather than risk presenting faulty histories, we decided to confine the description to a snapshot taken in 1981, the time of the last survey. Occasionally we have relevant data collected from the men at an early point in their lives—age fifteen—before the veterans entered the service and will use these data to examine whether military service helped develop veterans' personalities.

Tables 5-1 through 5-3 present the physical-, social-, and psychological-health status of the three matched groups of veterans and nonveterans at age thirty-six. To simplify the presentation, we have dichotomized each health-status indicator according to whether a problem is indicated. The tables present the percentage in each group with the problem; the higher the reported per-centages, the worse off the group, considered as a whole.

Physical-Health Status of the Groups

Table 5-1 gives data on the physical-health status of the matched groups. While proportionately more Vietnam veterans had a long-term health problem or disability, the groups did not differ significantly in terms of self-ratings of general health in the last three years. Contrary to popular belief, no significant group

Table 5-1
Indexes of Physical Health, 1981

Problem Relating to Physical Health	Vietnam Veterans	Non-Vietnam Veterans	Nonveterans	Is Group Difference Significant?
General health				
General health in last three years other than good	8.2%	6.6%	10.7%	No
Ill for more than seven days in past year	11.2	9.8	8.9	No
Long-term health problem or disability	22.7	17.7	15.2	Yes*
Health problem that limits work or activity	11.2	7.8	6.5	No
Substance use or abuse				
Cigarette consumption: Smoking over a half-pack a day	39.5	37.4	37.5	No
Alcohol consumption: Drinking heavily (at least one six-pack of beer or one bottle of wine or five drinks of liquor) at least once a month	43.8	40.1	38.7	No
Drug consumption: Ingesting following drugs every few months or oftener:				
Pain medication	55.3	54.1	53.0	No
Marijuana and other street drugs	9.2	8.1	6.5	No
Tranquilizers	4.7	2.7	4.0	No
Prescription stimulants	3.3	2.2	1.1	No
Sedatives, sleeping pills	2.2	2.9	1.3	No
Nonprescription stimulants	2.0	1.6	0.3	No
Narcotics	0.8	1.7	0.8	No
Sleep-related problems				
Reporting having following problems in past year:				
Difficulty sleeping	38.8	35.6	33.5	No
Sleep disturbed by troubling thoughts	34.9	29.6	27.8	No
Difficulty getting up in morning	21.5	20.2	24.8	No
Nightmares	20.7	12.4	13.5	Yes**
Average year sleep-related problem(s) started	1970	1972	1971	No

*Significant at 0.05 level.
**Significant at 0.01 level.

differences in cigarette, alcohol, or drug consumption were found, although there was a tendency for Vietnam veterans to report slightly greater usage. A significantly greater proportion of Vietnam veterans reported being troubled by nightmares. The average year of onset of these sleep-related problems was 1970, a couple of years or so following the soldiers' return from Vietnam.

Social-Health Status of the Groups

Table 5-2 presents data on the social-health status of the matched groups. A pattern similar to that reported for physical health was found. In general, Vietnam veterans reported the greatest number of social-interaction problems and antisocial behaviors, but few of these group differences reached statistical significance. In short, although the Vietnam-veteran group was slightly more troubled socially than the other two groups, the general pervasiveness and severity of the problem was at a low level. The only group differences that did reach statistical significance concerned problems dealing with being convicted of a misdemeanor or felony at least once since 1960, getting along with wife or girlfriend, and having someone to whom one could feel emotionally close. The last group difference was the only one that could be called striking: 43.7 percent

Table 5-2
Indexes of Social Health, 1981

Problem Relating to Social Health	Vietnam Veterans	Non-Vietnam Veterans	Nonveterans	Is Group Difference Significant?
Social-interaction problems: Having following problems in past year:				
Getting on track in life	45.2%	39.4%	43.0%	No
Having someone emotionally close to	43.7	31.6	29.0	Yes***
Getting along with wife or girlfriend	42.6	36.6	33.4	Yes*
Enjoying free time and recreation	36.2	32.7	38.3	No
Getting along with family	26.4	23.4	24.8	No
Getting along with friends	22.2	19.2	17.0	No
Enjoying sex	15.6	15.0	14.4	No
Antisocial behavior				
Three or more traffic tickets since 1960 (excluding parking tickets)	46.4	43.9	44.0	No
Having been arrested at least once since 1960	26.7	25.7	22.7	No
Having been convicted at least once since 1960	16.0	13.3	9.4	Yes*

*Significant at 0.05 level.
***Significant at 0.001 level.

of Vietnam veterans felt that they had this problem. Comparable figures for the matched groups of non-Vietnam veterans and nonveterans were 31.6 percent and 29.0 percent, respectively.

In general the non-Vietnam veterans were more similar to the nonveterans than to the Vietnam veterans, a pattern quite different from that for the groups' educational and career achievement. This is the first indication that education and work achievement are shaped by the military experience but that postservice personal and social problems flow from serving in a war zone and not from the military-service experience alone.

Psychological-Health Status of the Groups

The groups were compared on several indexes of psychological health: alienation, anxiety, hostility, and depression. The first variable was measured by nine attitudinal items forming an alienation or social-isolation scale (Neal and Groat 1974; Dean 1961). Respondents were asked to indicate the extent to which they agreed or disagreed with the following statements: (1) Sometimes I feel all alone in the world; (2) There are few dependable ties between people anymore; (3) People are just naturally considerate and helpful; (4) The world we live in is basically a friendly place. (5) Most people are not really sincere in their relations with others. (6) The way things are now, a person has to look out pretty much for himself. (7) Most married people in our country lead trapped and frustrated lives. (8) Real friends are as easy to find as ever. (9) Most people seldom feel lonely. High alienation was indicated by agreement with statements 1, 2, 5, 6, and 7 and by disagreement with statements 3, 4, 8, and 9.

Anxiety, hostility, and depression were measured by asking respondents to indicate the extent to which they were distressed in the past year (not at all; somewhat; quite a bit) by the behaviors listed in table 5-3.[1]

Table 5-3 shows that there were no significant group differences in alienation or hostility. Vietnam veterans, however, once again exhibited a pattern of slightly higher scores on these characteristics, compared to their former classmates. Larger, significant group differences in anxiety and depression were found, with Vietnam veterans consistently reporting the highest levels of distress. Relative to their former classmates, Vietnam veterans were especially bothered by the following indicators of anxiety—being easily startled by random noises, feeling fearful for no apparent reason—and by the following indicators of depression—feeling lonely, feeling things won't be better tomorrow.

As was the case with physical- and social-health status, there was no indication that veterans who served outside the Vietnam fire zone were any worse off than their former classmates who never served in the military. All psychological problems were confined to the group of veterans who served in Vietnam.

Table 5–3
Indexes of Psychological Health, 1981

Problem Relating to Psychological Health	Vietnam Veterans	Non-Vietnam Veterans	Nonveterans	Is Group Difference Significant?
Alienation				
Average score, total scale[a]	23.07	22.76	22.59	No
Anxiety				
Average score, total scale[b]	7.86	7.28	7.35	Yes**
Percent reporting being distressed in past year by:				
Feeling restless or jittery	60.2	55.1	60.2	No
Feeling tense	57.7	54.3	57.3	No
Feeling nervous	52.4	47.2	48.3	No
Easily startled by random noises	40.7	21.9	19.3	Yes***
Feeling fearful for no apparent reason	31.0	24.0	22.4	Yes*
Hostility				
Average score, total scale[c]	6.95	6.75	6.84	No
Percent reporting being distressed in past year by:				
Letting little things anger you	62.4	60.7	61.4	No
Arguing a lot	44.2	40.7	45.3	No
Inability to control temper	26.4	20.4	25.3	No
Wanting to destroy things	23.5	21.8	16.8	No
Wanting to hurt people	16.3	11.3	10.7	No
Depression				
Average score, total scale[d]	6.98	6.58	6.61	Yes*
Percent reporting being distressed in past year by:				
Inability to get excited	46.4	37.6	40.9	No
Feeling lonely	43.1	32.8	34.3	Yes**
Feeling things won't be better tomorrow	36.7	27.7	32.6	Yes*
Feeling nobody cares	28.1	24.8	22.7	No
Feeling life not worth living	16.7	12.7	12.5	No

Source: From Derogatis and Cleary (1977); Derogatis, Rickels, and Rock (1976).
[a]Range = 9 to 36; standard deviation = 4.51; coefficient alpha reliability = 0.74
[b]Range = 5 to 15; standard deviation = 2.27; coefficient alpha reliability = 0.82
[c]Range = 5 to 15; standard deviation = 1.86; coefficient alpha reliability = 0.71
[d]Range = 5 to 15; standard deviation = 1.99; coefficient alpha reliability = 0.71
*Significant at 0.05 level.
**Significant at 0.01 level.
***Significant at 0.001 level.

Interaction with Health Professionals

Proportionately more veterans than nonveterans sought professional help for problems relating to alcohol and drug abuse (table 5–4). These problems were clearly traceable to the military-service stint. When veterans were asked what

Table 5–4
Interaction with Health Professionals, 1981

Index of Interaction with Health Professionals	Vietnam Veterans	Non-Vietnam Veterans	Nonveterans	Is Group Difference Significant?
Interaction with therapist or counselor: Sought help in last fifteen years for problems relating to:				
Marital or job adjustment	20.1%	17.7%	19.2%	No
Alcohol or drug use	4.9	5.3	1.6	Yes*
Nervous condition	9.8	7.8	6.0	No
Other mental-health problem	2.6	4.3	2.8	No
Hospitalization: Hospitalized in last fifteen years for problems relating to:				
Marital or job adjustment	2.4	0.9	1.7	No
Alcohol or drug use	3.1	2.8	1.5	No
Nervous condition	2.3	2.0	1.6	No
Other mental-health problem	1.0	0.7	1.6	No

*Significant at 0.05 level.

their alcohol- and drug-consumption levels were before and during service, 54 percent reported greater consumption of alcohol during service than before, and only 8 percent reported drinking less during service than before; 13 percent reported greater use of nonpharmacy drugs during service than before, and only 1 percent reported lower drug use during service than before. This pattern of heavier alcohol and drug consumption during service compared to before was found in both the Vietnam-veteran and non-Vietnam-veteran groups. The percentage of men who increased their base rate of alcohol consumption while in the service was similar in both veteran groups. A greater proportion of Vietnam veterans, however, increased drug ingestion while in the service (18 percent, compared to 10 percent of non-Vietnam veterans).

There were no significant group differences in terms of the proportion of each of the three study groups hospitalized for a social or psychological problem. There was, however, a tendency for a relatively greater proportion of Vietnam veterans to have been hospitalized for most of the problems studied: marital or job adjustment, alcohol or drug use, and a nervous condition.

Attribution of Social and Psychological Problems to the Military Experience

Veterans reporting problems relating to interaction with other people, anxiety, hostility, and depression were asked if they felt that these problems were caused or made worse by their military experience. The proportions of Vietnam veterans and non-Vietnam veterans responding affirmatively are presented in table 5-5. Differences between the two veteran groups were striking; many more Vietnam veterans than non-Vietnam veterans believed that the service was responsible for their problems. These perceptions are probably correct. Data previously discussed seem to indicate that the military experience was responsible for increased substance use and abuse but that only the specialized Vietnam experience was responsible for later problems relating to social interaction and to psychological health.

Table 5-5
Attribution of Social and Psychological Problems to the Military Experience, 1981

Problem	Among Those with Problem, Percent Feeling Problem Was Caused or Made Worse by Military Experience		Is Group Difference Significant?
	Vietnam Veterans	Non-Vietnam Veterans	
Social-interaction problems			
Getting on track in life	34.1	17.9	Yes**
Getting along with wife or girlfriend	33.6	10.6	Yes***
Having someone emotionally close to	32.2	7.4	Yes***
Getting along with friends	29.3	9.9	Yes**
Enjoying free time and recreation	27.0	7.7	Yes***
Getting along with family	21.6	10.7	No
Enjoying sex	15.1	4.3	No
Anxiety-related problems			
Easily startled by random noises	75.0	30.5	Yes***
Feeling nervous	43.9	14.9	Yes***
Feeling fearful for no apparent reason	41.9	10.4	Yes***
Feeling restless or jittery	39.6	17.3	Yes***
Feeling tense	33.6	13.7	Yes***
Hostility-related problems			
Wanting to hurt people	42.1	35.7	No
Wanting to destroy things	36.1	24.6	No
Inability to control temper	31.6	17.7	No
Letting little things anger you	31.2	17.4	Yes**
Arguing a lot	27.9	11.8	Yes**
Depression-related problems			
Feeling life not worth living	40.7	16.2	Yes*
Feeling lonely	37.6	11.8	Yes***
Feeling nobody cares	34.6	16.8	Yes*
Inability to get excited	28.3	17.2	No
Feeling things won't be better tomorrow	28.3	13.4	Yes*

*Significant at 0.05 level.
**Significant at 0.01 level.
***Significant at 0.001 level.

Personality and Changes in Personality

In the 1981 survey, respondents were asked to rate themselves on thirteen traits in comparison to other American men of their age: interest in being with other people, sensitivity to other people's needs, impulsiveness, energy, calmness, tidiness, interest in cultural activities, leadership capacity, self-confidence, maturity, self-reliance, capacity to tolerate stress, and capacity to adapt to change. A score of 1 was given to a self-rating of "much less than others," 2 to "somewhat less than others," 3 to "about the same as others," 4 to "somewhat more than others," and 5 to "much more than others." Average self-ratings given by each of the three groups are presented in the top half of table 5-6.

The highest self-ratings were given by non-Vietnam veterans, demonstrating the potentially positive consequences of military service for personality development. Three of the group differences were of a magnitude reaching statistical significance: interest in being with people, sensitivity to other people's needs, and interest in cultural activities. On each of these traits, highest self-ratings were given by non-Vietnam veterans, lowest by Vietnam veterans. These findings indicate that the personal aftermath of military service can vary tremendously depending on whether one was assigned to a combat zone.

Did military service really change the non-Vietnam veterans more than their classmates, or might the non-Vietnam veterans have been more interested in other people, more energetic, more mature, and so forth to begin with? The answer to this question is contained in the bottom half of table 5-6. In 1960 when the men were fifteen year olds attending the ninth grade, they were asked to describe themselves on the first ten of the personality traits. These early personality scores were not comparable to those obtained in 1981 because the former were gleaned from answers to many different questions (as opposed to a single item) and therefore encompassed a wider range of scores (0 to 24 instead of 1 to 5). To make the two sets of scores somewhat more comparable, each 1960 score was changed into a quintile score, with 1 standing for a score in the lowest fifth of the class and 5 for a score in the highest fifth of the class. Respondents' 1960 scores were then subtracted from their 1981 scores on the corresponding trait. Results from the subtraction are given in the bottom half of table 5-6.

Because of the arithmetical manipulations done with the 1960 scores, the change scores cannot be interpreted literally. They have meaning only in a relative sense; a large positive score relative to the two comparison groups indicates relatively more-positive personality change in the twenty-one-year period between age fifteen and age thirty-six. In general, the largest positive-change scores were obtained by the non-Vietnam-veteran group. This was especially true for the trait labeled sensitivity to other people's needs, followed by the traits labeled interest in being with people, tidiness, leadership, and maturity. We conclude that military service can and does lead to personality development if such service takes place outside a war zone.

Table 5-6
Personality and Changes in Personality

Personality Trait	Average Score			Is Group Difference Significant?
	Vietnam Veterans	Non-Vietnam Veterans	Nonveterans	
Personality self-ratings, 1981[a]				
Interest in being with people	2.84	3.04	2.98	Yes**
Sensitivity to other people's needs	3.42	3.72	3.53	Yes***
Impulsiveness	2.96	3.00	2.89	No
Energy	3.37	3.48	3.41	No
Calmness	3.24	3.35	3.24	No
Tidiness, neatness	3.39	3.46	3.37	No
Interest in cultural activities	2.74	2.92	2.84	Yes*
Leadership	3.62	3.64	3.62	No
Self-confidence	3.64	3.68	3.68	No
Maturity	3.65	3.73	3.64	No
Self-reliance	3.89	3.90	3.81	No
Capacity to tolerate stress	3.70	3.74	3.65	No
Capacity to adapt to change	3.75	3.79	3.68	No
Change in personality, 1960 to 1981[b]				
Interest in being with people	−0.09	0.10	0.04	No
Sensitivity to other people's needs	0.57	0.80	0.64	Yes*
Impulsiveness	0.06	0.08	−0.05	No
Energy	0.43	0.53	0.50	No
Calmness	0.46	0.51	0.36	No
Tidiness	0.61	0.73	0.58	No
Interest in cultural activities	−0.23	−0.09	−0.21	No
Leadership	0.60	0.71	0.57	No
Self-confidence	0.62	0.65	0.70	No
Maturity	0.79	0.88	0.74	No

[a] 1 = much less than other American men my age; 5 = much more.

[b] Computed by subtracting the respondent's 1960 quintile scale score on the trait (1 = score in the lowest fifth of the class; 5 = highest fifth) from his 1981 single-item self-rating (1 = much less than other American men my age; 5 = much more)

*Significant at 0.05 level.

**Significant at 0.01 level.

***Significant at 0.001 level.

Recapitulation and Integration: Posttraumatic Stress Disorder (PTSD)

As a group, Vietnam veterans are more troubled than carefully selected, matched groups of non-Vietnam veterans or nonveterans. Some of the group differences, attributable to the military experience, are small in terms of prevalence and severity—for example, differences in substance use and abuse at midlife. Other group differences, attributable to the Vietnam experience in particular, are relatively larger. Vietnam veterans report many more problems relating to nightmares, panic attacks, emotional numbing, withdrawal from the external environment, hyperalertness, anxiety, and depression than do their classmates who never served in Vietnam. These larger differences correspond almost perfectly to the disorder labeled posttraumatic stress syndrome (PTSD) by the American Psyciatric Association (Diagnostic and Statistical Manual, edition III, 1980). The manual lists four indicators of PTSD:

1. "Exposure to recognizable stressor or trauma."
2. "Reexperiencing of trauma through flashbacks, nightmares, or intrusive memories."
3. "Emotional numbing to or withdrawal from external environment."
4. "The experience of at least two symptoms from a list including hyperalertness, sleep disturbance, survival guilt, memory impairment, and avoidance of situations that may elicit traumatic recollections."

In one sense PTSD is a new disorder, having been officially recognized as a legitimate diagnostic category only recently. Barret-Ruger and Lammers (1981) trace the historical evolution of the official definition of the disorder. In the original *Diagnostic and Statistical Manual* of the American Psychiatric Association (DSM I), developed in 1952, combat stress was categorized under the heading gross stress reaction. In the DSM II (1968), the gross-stress category was deleted and combat stress was mentioned only in the context of the category "adjustment reactions of adult life." It was not until the DSM III (1980), on the recommendation of veteran task forces, that the new, specialized category PTSD was developed in order to diagnose combat-stress disorders.

This is not to say that PTSD is without historical antecedent. World War II veterans were known to suffer from "battle fatigue," World War I veterans from "shell shock." PTSD is thus an important combat-related variable to study because some version of the disorder has been known to plague a proportion of veterans after every war.

The remainder of this chapter focuses on an in-depth investigation of the incidence and severity of PTSD among Vietnam veterans and on the antecedents and correlates of this disorder. Are proportionately more Vietnam veterans than non-Vietnam veterans or nonveterans afflicted with PTSD more than a decade after exposure to the trauma of combat? If so, what is the magnitude of the group difference? How many more Vietnam veterans are afflicted, relative to their former classmates who did not have to fight a war? What background factors, military experiences, and combat experiences are associated with a relatively high probability of suffering from PTSD at age thirty-six? How is PTSD related to other areas of life functioning, such as educational and occupational attainment, absence from work, substance use and abuse, brushes with the law, contact with a counselor for help with problems, and hospitalization for other-than-physical problems? Does having PTSD increase the likelihood of an unfavorable evaluation of the service experience, ten to fifteen years after the experience has had an opportunity to gel?

First we define PTSD in operational fashion; we translate each of the four defining characteristics of the disorder into indicators available from our survey questionnaire. Although we cannot come up with a flawless operational definition of the disorder, we have sufficient information to come up with a satisfactory one.

Exposure to recognizable stressor or trauma: Proportionately more Vietnam veterans than non-Vietnam veterans or nonveterans were exposed to a recognizable stressor or trauma: live combat. In addition, it is at least theoretically possible that overseas military service, even outside a war zone, was traumatic for some non-Vietnam veterans. McDermott (1981) proposes that overseas service could be associated with a variety of stressors such as new and deficient diets, housing, and medical care; extreme weather conditions; loneliness; culture shock; and so forth. If the McDermott hypothesis is correct, then the incidence and severity of PTSD in the non-Vietnam-veteran group should fall somewhere in between the Vietnam-veteran and nonveteran groups. We use membership in the three study groups as a rough indicator of degree of exposure to a recognizable stressor or trauma.

Reexperiencing of trauma through flashbacks, nightmares, or intrusive memories: The survey questionnaire contained a direct question concerning the frequency of nightmares in the past year. There were no direct questions about problems relating to flashbacks or intrusive memories; however, three items related to what might be called loss of control, a concept with some overlap with flashbacks and intrusive memories. The items referred to the amount of distress in the past year caused by wanting to break or destroy something, by feeling fearful or apprehensive for no apparent reason, and by being unable to control one's temper. Answers to these four questions were treated as indicators of the reexperiencing of the trauma.

Emotional numbing to or withdrawal from the external environment: There were two indicators of emotional numbing and two indicators of withdrawal from the environment available from the questionnaire: the amount of distress in the past year caused by being unable to get excited about things, the extent to which having someone to be emotionally close to was a problem in the past year, the amount of distress in the past year caused by feeling that life was not worth living, and a self-rating of one's interest in being with people, relative to other American men of one's age. Answers to these four items were treated as indicators of emotional numbing and withdrawal.

PTSD-related symptoms, including hyperalertness, sleep disturbance, survival guilt, memory impairment, and avoidance of situations that may elicit traumatic recollections: No questionnaire items dealt with survivor guilt, memory impairment, or avoidance of situations eliciting traumatic recollections. Five items did concern hyperalertness or excessive jumpiness, and three dealt with sleep disturbance. These items were, respectively, the amount of distress in the past year caused by feeling restless or jittery, by letting little things make one angry, by feeling nervous, by feeling tense, and by being easily startled by random noises; and the frequency during the past year of episodes where one had difficulty sleeping, where one's sleep was disturbed during the night by troubling thoughts, and where one had serious difficulty getting up in the morning. Answers to these eight items were treated as indicators of the fourth set of PTSD-related symptoms.

Based on all of these available indicators, two PTSD scores were developed for each respondent:

1. A continuous PTSD scale score ranging from 16 to 80, indicating the severity of the disorder in each individual respondent.
2. A crude, dichotomous PTSD score with 0 indicating the absence of the disorder and 1 the presence of the disorder.

To be scored positive for PTSD, the respondent had to report having at least two symptoms from the list of four relating to reexperiencing of the trauma, two symptoms from the list of four relating to emotional numbing and withdrawal, and two symptoms from the list of eight relating to other, miscellaneous PTSD-related symptoms.

The continuous PTSD scale score had an acceptably high coefficient alpha index of reliability: 0.84. This finding indicates that the scale was internally consistent or homogeneous; that is, it likely was measuring a single disorder. The dichotomous PTSD score should be treated with greater tentativeness and caution. We use it as a crude indicator of the presence of PTSD. It should be remembered that our diagnosis was based on the reported presence of an imperfect list of symptoms in a research setting, as opposed to the established presence of a more-precise set of symptoms in a diagnostic setting.

Group Differences in the Severity and Incidence of PTSD

The first row of table 5-7 gives the average PTSD scale score for the three groups of men. As expected, Vietnam veterans had the highest score. Contrary to the McDermott hypothesis, there was no difference in the average score of the non-Vietnam-veteran and the nonveteran groups. The second row of the table shows that the same general finding is obtained when group differences in incidence, as opposed to severity, of PTSD are examined. Nineteen percent of Vietnam veterans have the disorder, according to our crude dichotomous index. The corresponding figure for the other two groups is one-third less (12 percent).

The main PTSD indicators separating the Vietnam veteran from the other two groups were those dealing with reexperiencing of the trauma (nightmares, loss of control) and those dealing with emotional numbing and withdrawal from the external environment. Group differences in the proportion within each

Table 5-7
Group Differences in PTSD, 1981

Index of PTSD	Vietnam Veterans	Non-Vietnam Veterans	Nonveterans	Is Group Difference Significant?
Average score, PTSD scale[a]	29.9	27.1	27.3	Yes***
Classified as positive for PTSD (at least two symptoms positive on subscales 1 and 2 and 3)	19.3%	12.9%	12.1%	Yes*
At least one symptom positive on PTSD subscale 1 (nighmares, panic attacks)	53.9	44.4	46.5	Yes**
At least one symptom positive on PTSD subscale 2 (emotional numbing, withdrawal from external environment)	69.7	61.4	64.0	Yes***
At least one symptom positive on PTSD subscale 3 (hyperalertness, excessive jumpiness, disturbed sleep)	87.1	83.8	86.4	No

[a]Range, 16 to 80; standard deviation, 9.67
*Significant at 0.05 level.
**Significant at 0.01 level.
***Significant at 0.001 level.

group reporting problems in these areas were quite significant. In contrast, group differences in the other miscellaneous PTSD symptoms (hyperalertness, excessive jumpiness, disturbed sleep) were insignificant.

Additional statistical tests confirmed that the Vietnam-veteran group was indeed significantly different from each of the other two groups in terms of PTSD severity, but the other two groups did not differ from each other on this variable. We infer from the pattern behind these results that in keeping with the residual-stress model of Figley (1978a) and contrary to the stress-evaporation model of Worthington (1977, 1978), PTSD problems stemming from the Vietnam conflict have persisted more than a decade after the traumatic experience; furthermore, increases in the baseline incidence and severity of PTSD are associated with the Vietnam experience but not with military service in general. Because of the latter conclusion, all further analyses of the antecedents and correlates of the disorder were confined to the sample of Vietnam veterans alone.

Antecedents of PTSD

There has been some disagreement in the literature about the relative contribution of background characteristics, general military adjustment, and the combat experience to the onset and persistence of PTSD. Proponents of the background or stress-predisposition model claim that those who succumb to the disorder had the predisposition to be broken by stress even before they entered the military. To a large extent, proponents of this background model also support the stress-evaporation model, which purports that most of the stress associated with military service evaporates with the passage of time (Worthington 1977, 1978; Carr 1973; Enzie, Sawyer, and Montgomery 1973; Borus 1974; Strange 1974). Their major evidential support for their models is that they have failed to find significant differences in postservice difficulties between soldiers who were assigned to Vietnam and their contemporaries who were not. In addition, within the group of Vietnam veterans, they have failed to find differences in postservice difficulties between veterans who saw heavy combat and veterans who did not. Finally, they have found that when help-seeking veterans are studied, their difficulties are at least as related to preservice difficulties as to the service or combat experiences. In general, this first group of studies has been hampered by a focus on very small, often self-selected, help-seeking samples, with a poorly chosen (and occasionally no) control group.

On the other side of the argument are those who claim that it is primarily the combat experience itself that triggers the onset of PTSD and that the disorder is long lasting: residual stress flows from combat many years after the combat experience has passed (Figley 1978a; Stampler and Sipprelle 1981; Barret-Ruger and Lammers 1981; McDermott 1981; Penk et al. 1981; Kadushin, Boulanger, and Martin 1981; Laufer et al. 1981; Strayer and Ellenhorn 1975; Figley and Eisenhart 1975). In support of their claims, these scholars cite research data showing that Vietnam veterans are more stressed than non-Vietnam veterans (a finding corroborated in the present study) and that, within the group of Vietnam veterans, those who saw heavy combat are more stressed than those who saw light or no combat. In general, these investigators have failed to find a relationship between preservice or service adjustment and postservice difficulties, although the Kadushin and Laufer investigations found that certain elements of an individual's background (such as being white and coming from a stable family) served to attenuate the negative effect of combat. This second group of studies has generally been more sophisticated than the first group in terms of sampling methods used; our data once again support the second group's point of view.

Table 5-8 presents the relationship between the presence of PTSD at age thirty-six among Vietnam veterans in our sample and a set of demographic, ability, and personality-background characteristics, a set of indexes of military adjustment, a set of other (noncombat) variables related to service, and a set of combat-related variables. Why do some Vietnam veterans develop PTSD while others do not? The data in table 5-8 seem to indicate that it is almost completely the intensity of the combat experience that determines who will come down with the disorder after the war is over and how severe the disorder will be. Fourteen background characteristics and eleven indexes of military adjustment and

Table 5–8
Antecedents of PTSD among Vietnam Veterans

Hypothesized Antecedents of PTSD	Was Variable Significantly Related to PTSD at Age Thirty-Six?	Direction Associated with High PTSD
Individual background characteristics, age fifteen		
Sociodemographic characteristics		
Race	No	
Socioeconomic status of parents	No	
Size of community of origin	No	
Academic ability	No	
Personality traits		
Interest in being with people	No	
Sensitivity to other people's needs	No	
Impulsiveness	No	
Energy, vigor	No	
Calmness	No	
Tidiness, neatness	No	
Interest in cultural activities	No	
Leadership capacity	No	
Self-confidence	Yes*	Low self-confidence
Mature personality	No	
Indexes of military adjustment		
Amount of liquor consumption during service	Yes*	High liquor consumption
Amount of drug use during service	No	
Disciplinary action during service	No	
Military awards	No	
Type of military discharge	No	
Other (noncombat) variables related to service		
Military rank	No	
Time spent in Vietnam	No	
Perceived cohesiveness of military unit	No	
Amount of trust in commissioned officers	No	
Amount of trust in noncommissioned officers	No	
Amount of trust in enlisted men	No	
Vietnam combat experience		
Receive fire from enemy	Yes**	Frequent exposure
Fire own weapon at enemy	a	Frequent exposure
Kill enemy	Yes*	Frequent exposure
See someone get killed	Yes*	Frequent exposure
See enemy wounded	Yes*	Frequent exposure
See American wounded	Yes*	Frequent exposure
See enemy dead	Yes**	Frequent exposure
See American dead	a	Frequent exposure

Table 5–8 continued

Hypothesized Antecedents of PTSD	Was Variable Significantly Related to PTSD at Age Thirty-Six?	Direction Associated with High PTSD
Find self in combat situation where survival was in jeopardy	Yes***	Frequent exposure
Receive injury	Yes*	Injury requiring hospitalization

aThis relationship with PTSD barely missed significance at the 0.05 level. It was significant at the 0.10 level.

*Significant at 0.05 level.

**Signfiicant at 0.01 level.

***Significant at 0.001 level.

service behavior were studied for their possible association with subsequent PTSD. Of these variables, only self-confidence at age fifteen and amount of liquor consumption during the period of military service were associated with PTSD at age thirty-six. The lower one's self-confidence as a teenager and the greater the amount of liquor consumed while in the service, the higher the probability of having PTSD-related problems at age thirty-six. It is impossible to establish from our data whether heavy liquor consumption was a precursor of PTSD (a behavior indicating susceptibility to breaking down under stress) or a consequence of ongoing combat-related stress problems.

In sharp contrast to the negative findings obtained with the background and military-adjustment variables, large, positive findings were obtained with the combat-experience variables. Ten combat experiences were studied for their possible association with subsequent PTSD (the nine items making up our combat scale plus an additional item on whether the respondent was injured during the Vietnam fighting). All were related to the disorder; the more severe the soldier's exposure to combat and injury during the Vietnam war, the greater the number of PTSD-related problems as a civilian citizen more than a decade later. We divided the Vietnam-veteran sample into those who had seen relatively heavy combat (those scoring in the top third of the combat scale) and those who had not. Incidence of PTSD was 27 percent in the former group, a figure significantly higher than either the 12 percent baseline figure in the non-Vietnam-veteran and nonveteran groups or the 19 percent figure in the Vietnam-veteran group taken as a whole.

The data, while correlational, are consistent with the conclusion that heavy combat has long-lasting effects on psychological health, imposing lingering stress on many soldiers' lives long after the combat experience.

Sociodemographic, Health, and Social Correlates of PTSD

How does PTSD affect other spheres of human functioning? We looked at the degree of association between PTSD and a gamut of indicators of performance in other dimensions of living, including marital status, educational achievement, occupational achievement, absence from work, substance use and abuse, brushes with the law, contact with a counselor for help with problems, hospitalization for other-than-physical problems, and the men's evaluation of the overall effects of military service on their subsequent lives. Results are given in table 5-9.

The presence of a significant association in the table does not imply that PTSD caused the problem (in technical terms, a significant correlation between two variables says nothing about the direction of causality between the variables). The relation between PTSD and its correlates is likely to be one of reciprocal causality; problems with one's spouse or work caused by PTSD exacerbate PTSD, which in turn leads to further problems with family and work, and so forth. The combat veteran is caught in a vicious cycle, contributing to the persistence of his problems through time.

Table 5-9 shows that a high PTSD score is significantly associated with living alone, and with divorced, separated, and single marital status. The direction of causality is not clear from our data. Does PTSD lead to marriage break-up, or does living alone, without the possibility of spousal support, heighten PTSD-related problems? In all likelihood, both forces are at work.

PTSD was very slightly associated with low educational attainment, but the disorder was not related to occupational attainment. This finding is consistent with the results presented in chapters 3 and 4 regarding the absence of a relationship between combat and subsequent socioeconomic achievement.

There was a clear and strong association between the presence of PTSD and the presence of other health and social problems. A high PTSD score was associated with missed days at work, relatively heavy drug consumption, relatively more-frequent arrests, with seeking professional help for problems, and with hospitalization for other-than-physical problems. PTSD was also strongly associated with the perception that military service had negative instead of positive effects on one's future life.

We conclude that the effects of PTSD spill over into other areas of human functioning in a manner that is inevitably unfavorable for many veterans' quality of life.

Table 5-9
Sociodemographic, Health, and Social Correlates of PTSD among
Vietnam Veterans

Hypothesized Correlate of PTSD (Measured Concurrently at Age Thirty-Six)	Was Variable Significantly Related to PTSD at Age Thirty-Six?	Direction Associated with High PTSD
Sociodemographic status		
Demographic characteristics		
Marital status	Yes**	Divorced, separated, single
Living with wife or girlfriend	Yes**	Not living with wife or girl-friend
Educational achievement		
High-school degree	No	
College degree	No	
Number of years of schooling completed	a	Low educational attainment
Occupational achievement		
Job prestige	No	
Hourly pay	No	
Yearly pay	No	
Health and social problems		
Absence from work		
Days ill	Yes**	Relatively high absenteeism
Substance use and abuse		
Cigarette consumption	No	
Liquor consumption	No	
Drug consumption		
Pain medication	No	
Tranquilizers	a	Relatively heavy consumption
Sedatives, sleeping pills	a	Relatively heavy consumption
Prescription stimulants	Yes***	Relatively heavy consumption
Nonprescription stimulants	Yes**	Relatively heavy consumption
Narcotics	Yes*	Relatively heavy consumption
Marijuana and street drugs	Yes*	Relatively heavy consumption
Brushes with the law		
Traffic tickets	No	
Arrests	Yes*	Having been arrested
Felonies	a	Having been convicted
Contact with counselor for problems		
Marital or job adjustment	No	
Alcohol or drug use	Yes*	Having sought help for this
Nervous condition	Yes***	Having sought help for this
Other mental health problem	Yes*	Having sought help for this
Hospitalization for problems		
Marital or job adjustment	Yes*	Having been hospitalized for this
Alcohol or drug use	Yes*	Having been hospitalizaed for this
Nervous condition	No	
Other mental-health problem	No	

Table 5-9 continued

Hypothesized Correlate of PTSD (Measured Concurrently at Age Thirty-Six)	Was Variable Significantly Related to PTSD at Age Thirty-Six?	Direction Associated with High PTSD
Evaluation of overall (positive or negative) effects of service	Yes**	Perception that service had negative effects for one's future

aThis result barely missed significance at the 0.05 level. It was significant at the 0.10 level.
   *Significant at 0.05 level.
  **Significant at 0.01 level.
 ***Significant at 0.001 level.

Variables Moderating the Incidence and Severity of PTSD

We investigated whether certain elements of the Vietnam-veterans' environment were associated with reduced levels of PTSD. Laufer and colleagues (1981) found that the association between combat and postservice stress was "confined mainly to veterans who served between 1968 and 1974" (p. 315), the latter years of the war. Kadushin, Boulanger, and Martin (1981) found that the presence of friends who are also Vietnam veterans "helps to reduce current levels of stress" (p. 477). Our 1981 questionnaire had information on when each Vietnam veteran served in Vietnam. Although we did not have information on the veteran's present friendship networks, we did have information on some potentially related aspects of social support: the size of the community in which the veteran was currently residing and the degree to which the veteran actively participated in five types of organizations: church, social organizations, civic organizations, professional organizations, and charitable organizations.

We performed a series of analyses of variance with these timing and environmental variables as independent variables, PTSD in its dichotomous and continuous form as the dependent variable, and amount of combat experienced in Vietnam as a covariate. We found only participation in church activities to be associated with reduced incidence and severity of PTSD.

Summary and Conclusions

Educational and work achievement are shaped by the military experience; the combat experience does not appear to affect these achievements directly. In contrast, evidence shows that postservice social and psychological problems flow from service in a war zone, not from the military experience itself. Those experiencing heavy combat are especially vulnerable to long-term psychological consequences.

In contrast, military service outside a war zone can and does contribute to personality development. The following traits are especially benefited: sensitivity to other people's needs, interest in being with people, tidiness, leadership, and maturity.

Military service during the Vietnam era was marked by relatively high levels of drug and alcohol consumption. This was true for soldiers stationed in Vietnam, as well as outside the war zone. These patterns of heavier-than-normal drug and alcohol consumption, however, for the most part were abandoned after the service stint. By age thirty-six, although veterans continue to report slightly higher ingestion rates than nonveterans, the differences are not statistically significant.[2]

Other group differences are relatively larger and longer lived. At age thirty-six, Vietnam veterans report significantly more problems relating to nightmares, loss of control over behavior, emotional numbing, withdrawal from the external environment, hyperalertness, anxiety, and depression. These problems correspond closely to the disorder labeled posttraumatic stress disorder by the American Psychiatric Association.

Our crude index of incidence of PTSD showed 19 percent of Vietnam veterans to be suffering from the disorder at age thirty-six. The corresponding figure for groups of non-Vietnam veterans and nonveterans matched on fifty-one preservice characteristics was 12 percent. We conclude that PTSD-related problems stemming from the Vietnam conflict have persisted a full decade after Vietnam veterans' return home from this conflict and that PTSD is associated with the Vietnam experience and not with military service in general. There is no difference in the prevalence or severity of PTSD in matched groups of non-Vietnam veterans and nonveterans.

Among Vietnam veterans, the primary antecedent of PTSD is the severity of the combat experience, not the background characteristics of the individual soldier or his general military behavior and adjustment. Twenty-seven percent of Vietnam veterans who experienced heavy combat manifest PTSD-related symptoms at age thirty-six.

PTSD is associated with other family, mental-health, and social-interaction problems, but we cannot prove that it causes these other problems. In all likelihood, reciprocal causal mechanisms are at work so that a problem in one area exacerbates problems in other areas.

Some environmental variables are associated with reduced levels of PTSD or with reductions in the degree of association between combat and PTSD. The presence of a spouse is an example, as is being a churchgoer. We cannot ascertain the direction of cause and effect from our data: whether these support factors reduce PTSD directly or whether veterans coming home with PTSD are incapable of seeking out these sources of support.

PTSD is not associated with subsequent occupational achievement, as indexed by income and by prestige of job held. This finding is consistent with that reported in chapter 4 concerning the absence of any association between the intensity of the combat experience and subsequent occupational attainment. Apparently a person can be troubled by combat-stress disorders and yet function competitively on the job. The strains become evident in nonwork-related areas of human functioning.

Discussion

For the most part, these findings and conclusions are consistent with those of other, large-scale studies of nationally representative groups of Vietnam veterans, non-Vietnam veterans, and nonveterans. We believe that the evidence is overwhelming that combat can and does lead to a syndrome of symptoms indicative of emotional distress and that the combat-induced distress often lasts a long time, certainly over a decade in many cases. More problematic is the establishment of the incidence of the disorder among combat veterans, relative to baseline, and of the extent to which environmental factors are capable of either preventing the problem or attenuating it, given that it occurs. The source of the difficulties in answering these questions is obvious.

Incidence is ideally established by trained professionals in a diagnostic setting. Self-reports to a mail questionnaire such as ours or even to personal interviews as in the case of the study by Laufer, Kadushin, and their colleagues, can arrive at only tentative diagnoses. Both our dichotomous index of PTSD and the Kadushin et al. dichtomous indicator of stress were based on arbitrary decision rules applied to a set of self-reported symptoms. In our case, the symptoms corresponded only imperfectly to the disorder-defining set, as given in the American Psychiatric Association's DSM-III manual. We said that the respondent suffered from the disorder if he reported having at least two symptoms indicative of each of three general indicators of PTSD. We could have set the criterion lower (requiring only one symptom from each indicator) or higher (requiring three). In the case of Kadushin and colleagues, a respondent was considered stressed if he scored in the top 20 percent of their respondents on a scale made up of twenty-three stress symptoms that had been mentioned 75 percent of the time in their review of the literature of traumatically stressed populations. They could have set their criterion lower (requiring a score in the top 30 percent to be considered stressed) or higher (requiring a score in the top 10 percent).

Similar problems of comparability apply to our definitions of heavy combat. We both defined heavy combat, arbitrarily, as a score in the top third of the respective combat scales. We could each have set the criterion higher or lower.

Although both of our combat scales consisted of checklists of combat-related behaviors engaged in while in Vietnam, the checklists were not identical.[3]

Our samples of Vietnam veterans were representative of a single grade cohort. Theirs were representative of the entire Vietnam-era fighting force. Our measures of emotional distress were taken in 1981, theirs in 1977 (for their northeastern sample) and 1978–1979 (for their South, Midwest, and West Coast samples).

Given all these points of departure, it is not surprising that our incidence figures are not identical. We found 19 percent of Vietnam veterans and 27 percent of Vietnam veterans who had experienced heavy combat to suffer from PTSD at midlife, compared to a baseline incidence of 12 percent (in non-Vietnam veterans and nonveterans). Kadushin and colleagues found the following proportions of stressed individuals in their Northeast sample: nonveterans, 14 percent; non-Vietnam veterans, 17 percent; Vietnam veterans, 21 percent; and Vietnam veterans who experienced heavy combat, 34 percent. Slightly higher proportions were found in their South, Midwest, and West Coast samples: 19 percent, 18 percent, 26 percent, and 35 percent, respectively (Kadushin, Boulanger, and Martin 1981, p. 534). Although the figures from the two studies are not identical, a pattern runs through them. The pattern is consistent with the conclusion that the military experience does not lead to long-lingering emotional distress but that heavy combat does; heavy combat doubles the risk of being in a state of emotional distress more than a decade after the combat experience.

What can be done to reduce such risk? Let us examine available evidence. We found married Vietnam veterans to have a lower PTSD incidence rate than other Vietnam veterans. Kadushin and colleagues found that it was having a supportive spouse, and not just being married, that counted. Kadushin and his colleagues also found that the timing of the homecoming made a difference, with combat being associated with later stress only for veterans who returned after 1968, when public attitudes toward the war had soured and the economy had worsened. We found no differences in the association between combat and PTSD that could be attributable to the timing of the homecoming, although we did find that Vietnam veterans who returned in the latter years of the war suffered occupational deficits. Kadushin and colleagues found a significant relationship between stress and minority status, low socioeconomic status, low educational attainment, and low occupational attainment. We did not replicate this finding. In our study, lack of self-confidence at age fifteen was the only background or achievement variable significantly associated with PTSD at midlife. Kadushin and colleagues found that having Vietnam-veteran friends in large cities and a community of Vietnam-veteran friends in small towns helped reduce combat-induced stress. We did not have data on friendship networks but did find church-going to be associated with lower levers of PTSD.

The evidence is again not as crisp and consistent as one might hope. Moreover, the data are primarily correlational (the Kadushin study did have retrospective

reports on earlier stress against which reports on current stress could be compared; our data were completely correlational). Nevertheless, a pattern does
emerge, one consistent with the conclusion that social support given to the
returning veteran can ameliorate long-lingering stress. The exact and optimal
form of this support is difficult to pinpoint with available data. Perhaps some of
the minor contradictions just described were caused by the fact that the type of
support that works is idiosyncratic to each returning combat veteran. But it
seems safe to say that a gamut of factors have helping potential: a friendly
homecoming, a supportive spouse, membership in a church, friends who are
Vietnam veterans. In the aftermath of a traumatic war, these sources of support
appeared to be of great help to many returning combat soldiers.

Notes

1. Items for these scales were adapted from the Brief Symptom Inventory
(BSI), a fifty-three-item self-report symptom inventory, which presents a list of
symptoms to subjects and asks them to note the extent to which they have been
bothered by each, on a five-point scale of distress ranging from "not at all" to
"extremely." Because anxiety, depression, and hostility were only three of over
a hundred variables measured by our survey questionnaire, the BSI was, for our
purposes, too lengthy to use without modification. We simplified it in three
ways: deleting some items, rewording others, and changing the five-point response scale to a three-point one. Because of these changes, our scales are no
longer comparable to the BSI or to its parent scales (the SCL-90-R and the
Hopkins Psychiatric Rating Scale). However, we acknowledge our historical debt
to these established scales and accept the limitations caused by our alterations.

In general, shortening a scale decreases its reliability. For purposes of this
study, however, we were willing to give up some total score reliability for
breadth of coverage of other constructs. Our empirical reliabilities were still
acceptably high (ranging from 0.71 to 0.82). Moreover, we were at least as
interested in the pervasiveness of each behavioral symptom used as an indicator
of anxiety, depression, or hostility as we were in the total score on the scales.
We included symptoms most strongly linked to combat in prior investigations in
our questionnaire.

2. Laufer et al. (1981) found, seemingly contrary to us, that "self-reported
drinking problems increase with exposure to combat" (p. 370). Further analysis
showed, however, "that this effect can be at least partially explained by differences in social background. When social background is controlled, the effects of
being in Vietnam and of exposure to combat are reduced and are not statistically
significant" (p. 370). Similarly, for drug use, "When effects of social background
and site are controlled . . . the differences . . . disappear" (p. 371). Our samples
of veterans and nonveterans were matched for social background, and we found

no statistically significant group differences, at age thirty-six, in veterans' versus nonveterans' patterns of substance use and abuse.

3. The combat scale of Kadushin, Boulanger, and Martin (1981) consisted of the following items: (1) was part of a land or naval artillery unit that fired on the enemy; (2) flew in aircraft over South or North Vietnam; (3) stationed at a forward observation post; (4) received incoming fire from enemy artillery, rockets, or mortars; (5) unit patrols encountered mines and booby traps; (6) unit received sniper or sapper fire; (7) unit patrol was ambushed; (8) unit patrol engaged the Vietcong (or guerrilla troops) in a firefight; (9) unit patrol engaged the NVA (organized military forces) in a firefight; (10) saw Americans killed or injured; (11) saw Vietnamese killed or injured; (12) killed anyone or thought you killed someone.

Respondents were asked how often they had experienced each activity— rarely, sometimes, often, or very often. The more frequent the reported experience, the higher the assigned score on the item. Complete details are given in Kadushin, Boulanger, and Martin (1981, pp. 670–671).

6

Family and Personal Life

This chapter explores three aspects of family and personal life. First, we examine the effects of military service on patterns of family formation and dissolution, including marriage, parenthood, separation, and divorce. Veterans and their matched group of former classmates are compared in terms of the age at which they first married, the number of children they have fathered by age thirty-six, and the frequency of break-ups of their marriages. Then we describe when important family-related transitions such as marriage and divorce tend to occur, relative to the period of military service.

Second, we look into whether there are differences in the extent to which veterans and their classmates currently enjoy life. We compare the three groups of veterans and nonveterans in terms of how they rate their present life on a ten-point scale where 1 is the worst-possible life and 10 the best-possible life, and how satisfied they are with eleven dimensions of life: relationship with wife or girlfriend, having and raising children, occupation, financial security and material well-being, health, relationship with relatives, relationship with friends, intellectual development, personal understanding and awareness, socializing and entertaining, and recreational activities. It is possible that with the passage of time, the more-immediate problems that veterans faced on their return from the service may have been erased. To test this possibility, reports of satisfaction with these eleven life dimensions obtained from respondents in 1974 are compared with present survey results.

Finally, we present an evaluation of the overall effects of military service, from the point of view of the veterans. Differences in the ways Vietnam and non-Vietnam veterans view their period of military service are described; the background and service-related factors associated with some veterans' feeling that service had a positive effect on their lives are also presented. Finally, the men themselves speak, describing the often-small, sometimes-great consequences of military service for their subsequent lives.

The data analyses in this chapter, as in the previous three chapters, were conducted on samples of Vietnam veterans, non-Vietnam veterans, and non-veterans, weighted so as to be matched on a wide gamut of preservice characteristics. The only exceptions are the tallies of responses to the open-ended questions on the effects of military service and of service in Vietnam, which were done without using case weights.

Family-Formation and -Dissolution Patterns

Group Differences in Marriage, Parenthood, Separation, and Divorce Patterns

Table 6-1 presents the family status of the three groups at age thirty-six. There were no significant differences in the groups' marital status (the proportions that were single, married, separated, divorced) or in the groups' household-composition patterns (the proportions living with wife or girlfriend, children, relatives, unrelated adults).

There were, however, significant differences in the ages at which the men started forming their families. Not surprisingly, since veterans were in the service during the prime family-forming ages for men, nonveterans began their families earlier. The average age of nonveterans at their first marriage was twenty-two and one-third, a year younger than non-Vietnam veterans and two years younger than Vietnam veterans. By age thirty-six, nonveterans had fathered more than two children on the average; veterans averaged fewer than two children. There were no group differences in the number of foster, step, or adopted children.

Viewed over the long run, military service does not appear to have had major impact on the break-up of families; there were no significant differences in the marital stability of the three groups. This was true for all indexes of marital stability investigated: average number of times married as of age thirty-six, average number of times separated, average number of times divorced, and percentage ever divorced. We tested the possibility that our failure to find significant group differences was an artifact brought about by the fact that the veterans had married later than the nonveterans and had therefore been exposed to the risk of divorce for fewer years. We reexamined group differences in the proportion ever divorced, controlling for age at first marriage and obtained the same conclusion.

Although group differences in marital stability were not large enough to reach statistical significance, the data suggested that overall, non-Vietnam veterans had the least-stable family lives. Relative to the other two groups, the non-Vietnam-veteran group had the smallest proportion married as of age thirty-six, had the largest proportion separated, had the largest proportion divorced, had the smallest proportion living with wife or children, had been married the greatest number of times, had been separated the greatest number of times, had been divorced the greatest number of times, had the largest proportion of individuals who had been divorced at least once, and had the smallest average number of children. None of these differences reached statistical significance, but the pattern is suggestive of small but possibly real differences in marital stability in a direction unfavorable to the non-Vietnam-veteran group. Why the interruptions caused by military service would affect the non-Vietnam-veteran group more adversely than the Vietnam-veteran group is unclear. Perhaps the greater physical and psychological needs of returning Vietnam veterans helped to keep some of their families together. The returning

Table 6-1
Family-Formation and -Dissolution Patterns

Variable Relating to Family Formation or Dissolution	Vietnam Veterans	Non-Vietnam Veterans	Nonveterans	Is Group Difference Significant
Marital status (percent)				No
Never married	7.6	6.4	5.4	
Married	82.9	80.8	84.9	
Separated	1.5	3.4	2.6	
Divorced or annulled	8.0	9.4	7.1	
Household composition(percent)				
Living with wife or girlfriend	86.1	85.1	86.3	No
Living with children	74.3	70.8	78.1	No
Living with other relatives	7.5	6.6	5.8	No
Living with unrelated adults	1.6	2.4	1.6	No
Variables relating to marriage				
Average age at first marriage	24.1	23.6	22.3	Yes***
Average number of times married	1.13	1.15	1.13	No
Variables relating to fatherhood				
Average number of natural children	1.87	1.74	2.12	Yes***
Average number of foster, step, or adopted children	0.21	0.24	0.21	No
Average total number of children	2.08	1.99	2.33	Yes**
Variables relating to marriage break-ups				
Average number of times separated	0.23	0.28	0.23	No
Average number of times divorced	0.27	0.30	0.26	No
Percent ever divorced (%)				
Unadjusted	21.0	28.0	25.0	No
Adjusted for age at first marriage	23.0	29.0	22.0	No

**Significant at 0.01 level.
***Significant at 0.001 level.

non-Vietnam veterans may have been freer to move on when marital problems occurred.

Service Exit and Family Transitions

Table 6-2 presents a descriptive picture of veterans' family-formation activities in the year of service exit and the four subsequent years. During these years, about half of the Vietnam veterans and half of the non-Vietnam veterans married or fathered a child.

Table 6-2

Family-Formation Activities in the Service-Exit and Four Subsequent Years

Year	Vietnam Veterans	Non-Vietnam Veterans	Is Group Difference Significant?
Marriages			
Service-exit year	8.8	8.9	No
First year after exit	15.7	18.9	No
Second year after exit	12.4	12.8	No
Third year after exit	5.0	7.3	No
Fourth year after exit	4.8	7.9	No
Children born			
Service exit year	6.8	7.4	No
First year after exit	12.3	10.9	No
Second year after exit	13.8	14.8	No
Third year after exit	13.2	14.6	No
Fourth year after exit	12.4	12.1	No

Note: Actual percentages may be higher than those reported because 2 percent of the study sample did not report dates of their marriages or children's births and percentages for children born were obtained from the 1974 TALENT survey and not from the 1981 survey (questions concerning dates of children's birth were not asked in 1981). Thus these percentages do not reflect the full spectrum of postservice births for men who exited from the service in the 1970s.

There was some activity revolving around family dissolution around this time, but such activity was weak compared to activity revolving around family formation (table 6-3). Around 8 percent of all veterans got divorced in the service-exit and four subsequent years. For non-Vietnam veterans, this proportion did not increase by much when analyses were restricted to men who were married prior to service entry (and who presumably were separated from their wives during the service years, putting potential strain on the marriage). For Vietnam veterans, however, this proportion increased significantly (to 12 percent) when only marriages begun before the Vietnam stint were examined. The increase was primarily attributable to the significantly higher divorce rate among Vietnam veterans, relative to non-Vietnam veterans, in the first year following service exit (5.6 percent versus 0.6 percent, respectively). The strain of separation, coupled with the relatively greater reentry adjustment problems of Vietnam veterans, were obviously too much for the marriages of a small subgroup of Vietnam veterans. One of every twenty marriages begun before the husband went to Vietnam was dissolved by divorce in this first year out of Vietnam. But after this first vulnerable year, Vietnam veterans' marriages were at least as stable as those of other veterans. By age thirty-six, there were no significant differences between the two veteran groups in terms of proportion who had been divorced at least once. The effect of Vietnam service appears to have been one of accelerating the break-up of marriages that would eventually have been dissolved, even without such service.

Table 6-3
Marriage Dissolution in the Service-Exit and Four Subsequent Years

Year	All Veterans			Veterans Married Prior to Service Entry		
	Vietnam Veterans	Non-Vietnam Veterans	Is Group Difference Significant?	Vietnam Veterans	Non-Vietnam Veterans	Is Group Difference Significant?
Separations						
Service-exit year	1.6	1.4	No	2.3	1.4	No
First year after exit	0.7	2.2	No	0.0	1.9	No
Second year after exit	0.6	1.1	No	0.7	0.0	No
Third year after exit	1.2	1.8	No	0.5	2.5	No
Fourth year after exit	1.4	1.7	No	0.4	0.0	No
Divorces						
Service-exit year	1.1	1.3	No	1.1	2.0	No
First year after exit	3.1	1.4	No	5.6	0.6	Yes*
Second year after exit	1.3	2.8	No	3.6	2.8	No
Third year after exit	1.2	1.4	No	0.0	1.8	No
Fourth year after exit	0.7	1.3	No	2.2	0.0	No

Note: Actual percentages may be higher than those reported because 2 percent of the study sample did not report dates of their separation or divorce.

*Significant at 0.05 level.

Satisfaction with Life

At the age of thirty-six, Vietnam veterans were the least satisfied with the overall quality of their lives; nonveterans were the most satisfied (table 6-4). When the men were asked to rate what they thought their lives would be like in five years, Vietnam veterans continued to show the most pessimism. In contrast, non-Vietnam veterans had caught up with and even surpassed the nonveteran group in terms of the future life satisfaction they expected. All groups' ratings for the future were more favorable than their respective ratings of the present. In short, relative to the other two groups, Vietnam veterans were dissatisfied with their present lives and pessimistic about the future. Relative to their own present state of well-being, however, Vietnam veterans, like the other two groups, were optimistic that their future would be brighter than their present.

In addition to asking respondents to rate the overall quality of their present and predicted future lives, the 1981 survey questionnaire asked respondents to rate their satisfaction with eleven dimensions of life that have been shown to be important determinants of life quality (Flanagan and Russ-Eft 1975): relationship with wife or girlfriend; having and raising children; occupation; financial security and material well-being; health; relationship with relatives; relationship with friends; intellectual development; personal understanding and awareness; socializing and entertaining; and recreational activities. There was a slight tendency for non-Vietnam veterans to report the highest satisfaction ratings, suggesting that these men's lives had completely returned to normal by 1981. On the whole, the group differences were small, with only one difference reaching statistical significance: satisfaction with one's current job or occupation. Vietnam veterans reported the lowest job satisfaction on this dimension, consistent with findings reported in chapter 4 concerning their relatively greater work-related problems.

The 1974 Project TALENT survey, in which all the men in the present study participated, asked respodents to rate their satisfaction with the same eleven dimensions of life. Table 6-4 shows the difference between the men's 1974 and 1981 ratings. For the most part, the change scores were positive; all groups were happier at age thirty-six than they were at age twenty-nine. The largest gains in satisfaction were found in the nonveteran group (for the dimensions relating to relationships with other people and to financial well-being) and in the Vietnam-veteran group (for the dimensions relating to occupation, health, socializing and entertaining, intellectual development, personal understanding and awareness, and recreational activities). The gains made by Vietnam veterans on the last three dimensions were significantly greater than the gains made by the other two groups. These results demonstrate that in the decade since they returned from the war, despite lingering social, psychological,

Table 6-4
Life Satisfaction and Changes in Life Satisfaction

Index of Life Satisfaction	Average Score			Is Group Difference Significant?
	Vietnam Veterans	Non-Vietnam Veterans	Nonveterans	
Rating of overall life, 1981[a]				
Life at present	7.09	7.32	7.49	Yes**
Expected life in five years	8.06	8.43	8.34	Yes**
Rating of satisfaction with eleven dimensions of life, 1981[b]				
Relationship with wife or girlfriend	4.02	4.13	4.11	No
Having and raising children	4.03	4.11	4.05	No
Occupation	3.68	3.86	3.83	Yes*
Financial security and material well-being	3.30	3.40	3.39	No
Health	4.08	4.12	4.05	No
Relationship with other relatives	3.79	3.78	3.68	No
Relationship with friends	3.84	3.90	3.85	No
Intellectual development	3.53	3.63	3.61	No
Personal understanding and awareness	3.80	3.91	3.82	No
Socializing and entertaining	3.31	3.43	3.37	No
Recreational activities	3.35	3.51	3.51	No
Changes in rating of satisfaction with eleven dimensions of life, 1974 to 1981[c]				
Relationship with wife or girlfriend	0.24	0.24	0.27	No
Having and raising children	0.21	0.08	0.27	No
Occupation	0.21	0.00	0.17	No
Financial security and material well-being	0.31	0.25	0.33	No
Health	0.26	0.25	0.25	No
Relationship with other relatives	0.36	0.29	0.42	No
Relationship with friends	0.16	0.13	0.26	No
Intellectual development	0.29	−0.05	0.05	Yes***
Personal understanding and awareness	0.19	−0.06	0.09	Yes**
Socializing and entertaining	0.48	0.31	0.40	No
Recreational activities	0.47	0.34	0.24	Yes*

[a]1 = worst possible life; 10 = best possible life.

[b]1 = very low; 5 = very high.

[c]4 = large change for the better; 0 = no change; −4 = large change for the worse.

*Significant at 0.05 level.

**Significant at 0.01 level.

***Significant at 0.001 level.

and job-related problems, Vietnam veterans have managed to make impressive strides in improving the quality of their lives.

The Overall Effects of Military Service

Our focus now turns to an evaluation of the overall effect of military service, from the point of view of the men. The 1981 survey asked each participating veteran, "What effect has military service had on your life?" Five response options were provided; "entirely positive effects," "mostly positive effects," "an equal balance of positive and negative effects," "mostly negative effects," and "entirely negative effects." The proportions of Vietnam veterans choosing the (entirely or mostly) positive, equally positive-negative, and (entirely or mostly) negative options were 0.56, 0.33, and 0.11, respectively. Corresponding proportions for the non-Vietnam-veteran group, matched with the Vietnam veterans on preservice characteristics, were 0.62, 0.30, and 0.07. Non-Vietnam veterans evaluated their military experience slightly more positively than did Vietnam veterans.

Antecedents of the Evaluation that the Service had Positive Effects

What background factors, military experiences, and Vietnam-related experiences were related to the overall perception that military service had had entirely or mostly positive effects on one's life? This question is important because of the sheer numbers of young men who give up some of the prime years of their life to serve their country in the military.

None of the background factors we looked at—race, socioeconomic status, or academic aptitude—was significantly related to the perception that military service had had an overall positive effect. There was a slight tendency for more nonwhites to be favorable about the military experience than whites (73 percent versus 61 percent, respectively), but the difference did not reach statistical significance. Location of service, if it was outside the Vietnam war zone, was also unrelated to perceptions of the effects of service. Groups of men serving in Asia (other than Vietnam), the United States, Europe, and the Middle East had approximately equal proportions of veterans who were satisfied with the service experience. Similarly, military-service branch did not have a significant impact, although there was a slight tendency for veterans who served in the army to look back with disfavor on their years of service, and for veterans who served in the navy to evaluate the service experience more positively.

All other variables characterizing the military experience were significantly related to subsequent evaluations of the overall effects of service. Men who enlisted willingly, who received at least one military award, who were never

Table 6-5
Background and Military-Experience Antecedents of Perception that Military Service Had Overall Positive Effects

Background and Military-Experience Variables	Was Variable Significantly Related to Perception That Service Had Positive Effects?		Subgroups Perceiving that Effects of Service Were:	
	Vietnam Veterans	Non-Vietnam Veterans	Positive	Negative
Background variables, age fifteen				
Race	No	No		
Socioeconomic status	No	No		
Academic aptitude	No	No		
Military-experience variables				
Mode of service entry	Yes***	Yes***	Enlisted willingly	Drafted; enlisted to avoid draft; other
Service branch	No	No		
Location of military service:				
Did person ever serve in:				
Asia, other than Vietnam	No	No		
United States	No	No		
Europe	No	No		
Middle East	No	No		
Receipt of military award	Yes*	No	Those with at least one award	Those with no award
Disciplinary action during service	Yes**	Yes*	Never formally disciplined	Disciplined at least once
Liquor consumption during service	a	Yes**	Not more than once a week	Several times a week or more
Drug consumption during service	a	Yes***	Not more than once or twice a month	Once a week or more

aBarely missed significance at 0.05 level. It was significant at the 0.10 level.
*Significant at 0.05 level.
**Significant at 0.01 level.
***Significant at 0.001 level.

formally disciplined while in the service, or who abstained from alcohol and drugs while in the service (or at least stuck to relatively low consumption levels) evaluated the service experience more favorably than men who were drafted or who enlisted solely to avoid the draft, men who were never the recipient of a military award, men who were formally disciplined at least once, and men who consumed relatively large quantities of alcohol and drugs while in the service. For the most part, these results were obtained in both the Vietnam-veteran and non-Vietnam-veteran groups (table 6-5).

In similar fashion, most of the Vietnam-experience variables investigated were significantly associated with subsequent evaluations of the service experience (table 6-6). The strongest association with positive evaluations was found among variables indicative of the trust and cohesiveness among the men in one's unit. Vietnam veterans who felt that the men in their unit were "extremely" or "very" close and who trusted their commissioned officers, noncommissioned officers, and fellow enlisted men "completely" or "a great deal" had much more positive evaluations of the service experience than Vietnam veterans who felt that their units were not so cohesive or trustworthy.

Those serving less than six months in the Vietnam fire zone evaluated the service experience more positively than those serving over six months. Commissioned and noncommissioned officers had more positive evaluations than enlisted men. Only two of the ten combat behaviors studied were significantly associated with later evaluations of the service experience: those who never saw an American wounded had more positive evaluations than those who had, and those who never saw Vietnamese dead had more favorable evaluations than those who had. In short, there was a slight tendency for lengthy and intense combat exposure to be associated with negative evaluations of the service experience, especially among enlisted men.

The Men Speak

After asking veterans what effects the military experience had on their lives, the survey questionnaire asked them to "explain your answer briefly, in your own words." In general, the men were quite responsive to this open-ended item. Of the 474 Vietnam veterans participating in the study, 393 (82.9 percent) gave at least one specific explanation for their rating, 38 (8 percent) gave a vague, uncodable answer (such as "no effect," "little effect," or "great effect"), and 43 (9.1 percent) gave no answer at all. Corresponding percentages among the 502 participating non-Vietnam veterans were similar: 406 (80.9 percent) with one or more specific answers, 50 (10.0 percent) with a vague, uncodable answer, and 46 (9.2 percent) with no answer ar all. The 799 veterans who gave responsive answers tended to have multiple explanations for their rating. The middle columns of tables 6-7 and 6-8 show that together these 799 men gave 1,351 reasons why the service experience was positive and 398 reasons why the service experience was negative. These reasons were typed (filling over one hundred pages) and then categorized into the positive effects given in table 6-7 and the negative effects of service given in table 6-8. Following are some typical responses, grouped according to whether the veteran's rating of the service experience was positive, neutral, or negative.

Rating of service: Entirely or mostly positive

Military experience gave me an academic education, managerial and professional experience, opportunity to travel, maturing process.

It made me realize my full potential as a man instead of that as a child. It also taught me a lot about working and to do the job right the first time.

Matured and became much more experienced via exposure to many people and societies. More disciplined. Developed strong personal relationships. Became more self-confident and self reliant. Trained me for future career.

Rating of service: Equal balance of positive and negative effects

Got to travel meet people and grow up. Definitely put me behind my peers financially.

Positive: Experience, insight, leadership skills, maturity, travel, exposure to other people's situations and problems, G.I. benefits. Negative: Lost time in career pursuits, lack of feelings of accomplishment.

I had career experiences I would not otherwise have had including exposure to having authority and responsibility. I enjoyed the travel and people I met. On the other hand I was very separated from normal society (esp. women) and career opportunities. So my income is not what it would have been, my social life has been slow to develop, but I have had experiences most people will never have.

Rating of service: Entirely or mostly negative

Broke up family unit. Started drinking. Worried about living every day. Killed a man.

For one, I did not or never will believe we ever belonged in Vietnam and the training and experience I gained in the Army was in no way beneficial to me.

I never drink to mount to anything after I went in service combat I had a hell experience which I will never forget. I wish that I could tell the world what really went on. This is what I got to live with. Please help me if you can. (We sent this individual a letter advising him to go to one of the VA Outreach Centers in his area of residence. We gave him the names, addresses, and telephone numbers of these centers.)

The answers given by Vietnam veterans and by non-Vietnam veterans were categorized and tallied separately. As a group, Vietnam veterans gave 646

Table 6-6
Vietnam-Experience Antecedents of Perception that Military Service Had Overall Positive Effects, Vietnam Veterans

Vietnam-Experience Variables	Was Variable Significantly Related to Perception That Service Had Positive Effects?	Subgroups Perceiving that Effects of Service Were:	
		Positive	Negative
Length of service in Vietnam	a	Those serving six months or less	Those serving over six months
Military rank in Vietnam	Yes**	Commissioned officers Noncommissioned officers	Enlisted men
Combat experiences			
Receiving fire from enemy	No		
Firing weapon at enemy	No		
Killing enemy	No		
Seeing someone killed	No		
Seeing enemy wounded	No		
Seeing American wounded	Yes*	Those who never experienced this	Those who experienced this
Seeing enemy dead	Yes*	Those who never experienced this	Those who experienced this
Seeing American dead	No		

Being in a situation where survival was in jeopardy	No		
Being injured	No		
Trained with Vietnam unit?	No		
Rating of cohesiveness of Vietnam unit	Yes***	Those feeling men in unit were extremely or very close	Those feeling men in unit were fairly close, not very close, or not close at all
Trust commissioned officers in unit?	Yes***	Those trusting commissioned officers completely or a great deal	Those trusting commissioned officers somewhat, not very much, or not at all
Trust noncommissioned officers in unit?	Yes***	Those trusting noncommissioned officers completely or a great deal	Those trusting noncommissioned officers somewhat, not very much, or not at all
Trust enlisted men in unit?	Yes**	Those trusting enlisted men completely or a great deal	Those trusting enlisted men somewhat, not very much, or not at all

aBarely missed significance at the 0.05 level. It was significant at the 0.10 level.

*Significant at 0.05 level.
**Significant at 0.01 level.
***Significant at 0.001 level.

Table 6–7
Classification of Veterans' Responses to Questions Concerning Effects of Military Service and of Vietnam on Their Lives: Positive Effects

Beneficial Effects	Effects of Military Service			Effects of Vietnam	
	Vietnam Veterans (N=474)		Non-Vietnam Veterans (N=502)		Vietnam Veterans (N=474)
	No. (%) Citing Effect		No. (%) Citing Effect		No. (%) Citing Effect
Relating to educational attainment	24 (5.1%)		42 (8.4%)		2 (0.4%)
Educational training in the service	12		23		1
Opportunity to use GI Bill to continue school after service	12		19		1
Relating to occupational and socioeconomic attainment	66 (13.9)		66 (13.1)		2 (0.4)
Job or professional training experience in service	49		54		0
High pay and good benefits in service	8		4		1
Miscellaneous veterans' benefits (such as housing)	9		8		1
Relating to physical health	39 (8.2)		72 (14.3)		0 (0.0)
Improved physical conditioning, poise, appearance	5		10		0
Improved sense of self-discipline, tidiness	34		62		0
Relating to social health	205 (43.2)		213 (42.4)		75 (15.8)
Opportunity to see the world	56		56		4
Expansion of horizons; development of appreciation	75		46		45

for other people and cultures			
Increased sensitivity; improved ability to get along with others	20	55	40
Improved leadership skills	3	28	18
Acquisition of new friends	3	28	16
Relating to personal growth and psychological health	129 (27.2)	234 (46.6)	255 (53.8)
Increased appreciation for the value of life, for what is important in life	58	10	23
General learning, maturing experience	31	119	125
Development of self-understanding	6	17	16
Development of independence, self-confidence	18	62	57
Feeling of personal accomplishment	2	3	3
Improved planning and goal-setting abilities	1	13	11
Improved ability to cope with stress	10	10	19
Positive religious outcomes	3	0	1
Relating to citizenship	62 (13.1)	20 (4.0)	27 (5.7)
Development of appreciation for the American way of life	46	5	13
Feeling of patriotism, of pride in having served one's country	16	15	14
Relating to life satisfaction	10 (2.1)	58 (11.6)	30 (6.3)
Enjoyable service experience	10	58	30
Total number of positive effects cited	280 (59.1)	705 (140.4)	646 (136.3)

Note: Multiple answers to both questions were allowed.

Table 6–8
Classification of Veterans' Responses to Questions Concerning Effects of Military Service and of Vietnam on Their Lives: Negative Effects

| | Effects of Military Service | | Effects of Vietnam |
| | Vietnam Veterans (N=474) | Non-Vietnam Veterans (N=502) | Vietnam Veterans (N=474) |
Negative Effects	No. (%) Citing Effect	No. (%) Citing Effect	No. (%) Citing Effect
Relating to educational attainment			
Educational deficits relative to peers	5 (1.1%)	9 (1.8%)	1 (0.2%)
	5	9	1
Relating to occupational and socioeconomic attainment	33 (7.0)	39 (7.8)	20 (4.2)
Occupational deficits relative to peers	16	23	10
Financial deficits relative to peers	6	9	1
Loss of achievement motivation	0	0	3
Experience of job discrimination upon return to civilian life	1	0	1
Problems with getting or holding jobs	1	0	3
Negative conditions in present job	8	6	1
Inadequate postservice disability benefits	1	1	1
Relating to physical health	17 (3.6)	13 (2.6)	21 (4.4)
Physical wounds, injuries	6	1	4
Drug problems	2	4	3
Alcohol problems	7	8	5
Nightmares and other sleep-related problems	2	0	9
Relating to social health	34 (7.2)	23 (4.6)	49 (10.3)
Anger, hostility, antisocial feelings	4	1	12
Cynicism, inability to make friends	8	6	24

Emotional numbing	2	0	0
Suffering associated with separation from home while in service	11	5	2
Current marital or family problems	8	7	7
Prejudice or uncaring for other people and cultures	1	4	4
Relating to personal growth and psychological health	24 (5.1)	23 (4.6)	56 (11.8)
Mental breakdown	4	0	5
Oversensitivity to noise	1	2	4
Nervousness, anxiety, fear	8	5	18
Depression	1	1	1
Feelings of guilt, shame, regret, disgrace	1	1	7
Problems with readjustment to civilian life, with coping with stress	9	14	21
Relating to citizenship	21 (4.4)	9 (1.8)	63 (13.3)
Target of civilian hatred or indifference	7	3	20
Loss of respect for the law	1	1	1
Loss of civic pride, of faith in America	13	5	42
Relating to life satisfaction	74 (15.6)	74 (14.7)	70 (14.8)
Waste of time, unwanted life interruption	22	24	16
Experience of grief at death, suffering	5	0	19
Degrading, humiliating service experience	9	8	0
Harassing, frustrating service experience	19	25	7
Impersonal service environment	1	4	0
Boring service experience	0	6	0
General expression of suffering during service experience	2	1	0
Experience of personal dissatisfaction, bitterness, sadness after service	16	6	27
Total number of negative outcomes cited	208 (43.9)	190 (37.8)	280 (59.1)

Note: Multiple answers to both questions were allowed.

responses that were categorized as positive and 208 responses responses categorized as negative. Non-Vietnam veterans gave 705 positive and 190 negative responses. Although both groups listed more positive than negative effects, the Vietnam-veteran group gave more negative responses and fewer positive responses than the non-Vietnam-veteran group. This is consistent with findings that the proportion in both groups rating the service experience as positive was much higher than the proportion rating the experience as negative; but ratings given by the Vietnam-veteran group were less favorable than comparable ratings given by the non-Vietnam-veteran group.

In both groups, the positive outcomes most frequently mentioned were related to personal growth and social-psychological health: increased maturity, independence, self-confidence; opportunity to see the world and expand one's horizons; development of appreciation for other people and cultures; and improved sensitivity and ability to get along with others. Another frequently mentioned positive outcome of service was the job or professional training provided by the service.

These occupational consequences were, however, a double-edged sword. On the one hand, many men appreciated the training they received in the service. On the other, one of the most frequently cited negative outcomes of military service was that it put veterans at an occupational disadvantage relative to their peers. The two other most frequently cited negative outcomes centered around the perception that service was a waste of time and an unwanted life interruption and the feeling that the service years were a particularly harassing and frustrating period in the men's lives.

The last item in the survey questionnaire asked Vietnam veterans, "Please tell us briefly, in your own words, how your experiences in Vietnam have affected your life." Responses are categorized in the last column of tables 6-7 and 6-8. In one sense, the men were not nearly as responsive to this item as to the one on the effects of military service. Of the 474 Vietnam veterans participating in the study, 33 (7.0 percent) gave no answer, 129 (27.2 percent) gave a vague, uncodable answer, and only 312 (65.8 percent) gave a specific, responsive answer. In contrast to the previous question, which generated 646 positive and 208 negative responses from Vietnam veterans, this question generated only 280 positive and 280 negative responses from the same men. We cannot be certain about the reasons behind the poorer rate of response to the second question. Perhaps the Vietnam veterans felt that they had already answered this question when they responded to the first question about the effects of military service; or, because this second open-ended question was the last one in a lengthy questionnaire, respondents had become tired by the time they got to this question; or, in keeping with findings reported by other investigators, Vietnam veterans do not like to talk directly about their experiences in Vietnam.

Regardless of the reason for the poor response rate, we can examine the answers that were provided to gain some insight into the special effects of service in Vietnam. A few answers, especially some negative ones, were notable for the amount of emotion they contained. In this sense, they were different from the more-matter-of-fact responses to the question on the effects of military service. Some examples illustrate the intense bitterness still felt by a small minority of Vietnam veterans:

> One year of intense emotions 10,000 miles from home. Lost chances for promotion at job. Returned home to find knowone gave a damn about the men who died. Whatever happened to "Welcome Home-G.I."—It turned into "Hell no we wont go."

> It taught me one hell of a lesson but what the hell, it was *only one (1) year of my life!* I'll *never* go again unless it's to defend the ground that I'm standing on! *This* in brief *is exactly the way I feel.* Some *fat cat* sat back—twiddled his thumbs and got rich from the boys (men) on the battlefield. Do you think for a minute that he cared?

> Being in Vietnam was the worst experience I have ever had. 99% of the men I served with, as did I, did not agree with our countries policies concerning it, and did not want to be there—it was a war we could not win and should never have been involved.

> I have confidence in my ability to live under practically any physical conditions if necessary and put up with whatever mental hardships that might occur. I have no ill effects from it to my knowledge but I can understand how people can have them, especially those exposed to great deal of combat and have returned to find great indifference to what they have been through.

Clearly the Vietnam experience was charged with more emotion than the general military experience.

The Vietnam experience seemed also to be generally more negative. Whereas Vietnam veterans' positive responses to the question concerning the effects of military service outnumbered their negative responses by a ratio of three to one, responses of the same men to the question on the effects of the Vietnam experience contained an equal proportion of positive and negative commnents.

Finally, the different content of the responses to the two questions can be examined to isolate some of the particular consequences of the Vietnam experience that distinguish it from the more-general experience of military service. To do this, we list the positive and negative categories that Vietnam veterans used more frequently in response to the question on the effects of the Vietnam experience (question 2) than in response to the question on the effects of military service (question 1). Because there were far fewer total responses to question 2, these categories can be viewed as indicators of consequences that were more characteristic of the Vietnam experience than of the general military experience.

Three positive effects were cited more frequently in response to question 2 than question 1. In order of decreasing salience to the unique Vietnam experience (with salience calculated as the difference between the number of citations, question 2, and the number of citations, question 1), they were:

1. Increased appreciation for the value of life, for what is important in life.
2. Development of appreciation for the American way of life.
3. Feeling of patriotism, of pride in having served one's country.

There were sixteen negative effects cited more frequently in response to question 2 than to question 1. In order of decreasing salience to the unique Vietnam experience, they were:

1. Loss of civic pride, of faith in America.
2. Cynicism; inability to make friends.
3. Experience of grief at death, suffering.
4. Experience of being a target of civilian hatred or indifference.
5. Problems with readjusting to civilian life, with coping with stress.
6. Experience of personal dissatisfaction, bitterness, sadness after service.
7. Nervousness, anxiety, fear.
8. Anger, hostility, antisocial feelings.
9. Nightmares and other sleep-related problems.
10. Feelings of guilt, shame, regret, disgrace.
11. Oversensitivity to noise.
12. Loss of achievement motivation.
13. Prejudice or uncaring for other people and cultures.
14. Problems with getting or holding jobs.
15. Mental breakdown.
16. Drug problems.

The Vietnam war, which polarized the country when it was at its peak, seems also to have polarized the soldiers who bore the brunt of the fighting. For some of these soldiers, greater pride in America was a unique legacy of having fought in the war; for others, loss of pride and faith in their country resulted from the same experience.

The other positive effect of Vietnam service that distinguished it from more-general military service was similarly of a very general nature. Many Vietnam veterans said that fighting in the battlefields and coming close to death led to an increased appreciation for the value of life and for what is important in life. These testimonials parallel those that have been elicited from men and women who have had other types of close brushes with death, stemming from a variety of sources, including physical illness, accidents, surgical complications, and even serious attempted suicides. Facing the prospect of death before one's normal, appointed time can make one appreciate life more and take less about life for granted.

In contrast to these few, broad positive effects of Vietnam service, the unique negative effects of the same experience were more numerous, as well as more specific in nature. Many of the negative effects centered on the persistence of symptoms associated with PTSD. The PTSD symptoms mentioned by the men as constituting unique, negative effects of the Vietnam experience were inability to make friends, nervousness, anxiety, fear, anger, hostility, antisocial feelings, nightmares and other sleep-related problems, oversensitivity to noise, and mental breakdown.

In addition to these PTSD symptoms, there were unique effects centering on negative emotions suffered both during the Vietnam stint itself (for example, the experience of grief at suffering and death), as well as after the stint (for example, the experience of personal dissatisfaction, bitterness, and sadness after the period of service in Vietnam, and feelings of guilt, shame, regret, and disgrace, often still felt up to the present time).

Other unique effects of the war experience had to do with heightened readjustment problems upon reentry into civilian life. Some of the readjustment problems the men mentioned were related to their jobs (loss of achievement motivation, problems with getting and holding jobs). Other reentry problems were more general in their nature (for example, the experience of being a target of civilian hatred or indifference and problems with coping with the stresses of civilian life).

In general, qualitative analyses of the men's feelings regarding their military experience yielded insights remarkably similar to those obtained from the quantitative analyses reported in prior chapters, lending credence to the personal, in addition to statistical, reality of these findings.

Summary and Conclusions

Veterans started forming their families at an older age than nonveterans because veterans tended to be in the service during the years when men typically start marrying and having children. By age thirty-six nonveterans had fathered over two children on the average, veterans under two. There were no group differences in marital status or in percentage ever divorced at this age. For Vietnam veterans, the one-year period following the service-exit year was a particularly vulnerable time for separation and divorce; for non-Vietnam veterans, no single period was marked by special vulnerability.

As a group, Vietnam veterans rated both their present life as well as their expected life in five years less favorably than non-Vietnam veterans or nonveterans. However, the only specific life dimension given a significantly lower satisfaction rating by Vietnam veterans than by their former classmates was job satisfaction. There were no significant group differences in satisfaction ratings assigned to ten other dimensions of life: relationship with wife or girlfriend, having and raising children, financial security and material well-being, health, relationship with relatives, relationship with friends, intellectual development, personal understanding and awareness, socializing and entertaining, and recreational activities. Non-Vietnam veterans had a slight tendency to give the highest satisfaction ratings to the set of dimensions but the size of the group differences was too small to be of practical significance.

Despite the relatively low life-satisfaction ratings given by Vietnam veterans, one cannot say that their life as a group did not improve in the decade since reentry into civilian life. When 1981 ratings on the eleven life dimensions were compared with similar ratings provided seven years previously (in 1974, when the men were twenty-nine years old), the Vietnam-veteran group exhibited the largest change for the better. Vietnam veterans' change scores in the areas of intellectual development, personal understanding and awareness, and recreational activities were significantly greater than similar change scores obtained for their former classmates.

In the 1981 survey, all veterans were asked to rate the overall effect of military service on their future lives. In the Vietnam-veteran group, 56 percent rated the experience as having "entirely or mostly positive effects," 33 percent as having "an equal balance of positive and negative effects," and ll percent as having "entirely or mostly negative effects." Corresponding figures for the non-Vietnam-veteran group were 62 percent, 30 percent, and 7 percent, respectively. In short, both groups rated the military experience as being more positive than negative, with the group of veterans who never had to fight a war being more positive on the average than the group who had to serve in the hostile fire zone.

The men were asked to explain their ratings in their own words, and their responses to this open-ended question were content analyzed (grouped into related categories and tallied). Their answers paralleled their numerical ratings. While both groups listed more positive than negative effects stemming from the service experience, the non-Vietnam veterans had more positive and fewer negative answers than the Vietnam veterans.

In both groups and especially the non-Vietnam-veteran group, the dominant positive outcomes centered on effects related to personal growth as well as increased social and psychological health, specifically increased maturity, independence, self-confidence; opportunity to see the world and expand one's horizons; development of appreciation for other peoples and cultures; and improved sensitivity and ability to get along with others. The dominant negative outcomes centered on the waste of time, as well as financial and job deficits brought about by the often-unwanted service interruption. In addition, the service period was a harassing and frustrating one for some of the men.

Vietnam veterans were asked a second open-ended question: to explain, in their own words, what effect service in Vietnam had on their lives. Their responses to this question were fewer in number but much more emotionally charged than their responses to the question concerning the effects of military service. In general the emotion was brought about by the extremely bitter feelings still held by some Vietnam veterans.

Negative effects of service in Vietnam (those answers cited more frequently in response to the question concerning Vietnam than in response to the question concerning the general military experience) focused on specific symptoms related to PTSD, such as nightmares, nervousness, and inability to become close to people; on the experience of much grief and sorrow during the combat period; and on negative feelings such as guilt, shame, and regret still felt up to the present time. Positive effects were fewer and of a more-general nature, focusing on a pride on the part of some Vietnam veterans at having served their country in a special way and on an increased appreciation for the value of life and for the things that are truly important in life.

We examined whether any particular background characteristics, military experiences, or combat experiences were associated with the later preception that, on the whole, service was a positive experience. We found no differences between whites and nonwhites or between men who were above versus below average in socioeconomic status or general academic aptitude. An equal proportion of these subgroups rated their military experiences positively. However, we found many military-experience variables to be linked to the later perception that service had an overall beneficial effect on one's life. Among these variables were willing participation in the service to begin with, receipt of a military award while in the service, never having been officially disciplined while in the service, and abstention from, or only light use of, alcohol and drugs while in the service. Among Vietnam veterans, additional factors associated with later favorable perceptions of the service were a short duty stint inside the war zone, relatively light combat experience (specifically, not having seen Americans wounded or Vietnamese killed), officer (as opposed to enlisted-man) status, and the perception that one's unit in Vietnam was cohesive and made up of trustworthy commissioned officers, noncommissioned officers, and enlisted men.

Overall, one is impressed not by the commonality but rather by the variance in the men's reactions to a common experience. A majority of the veterans, especially the non-Vietnam veterans, found the service experience worthwhile. Vietnam veterans were more polarized in their perceptions of the relative benefits versus costs of their service stint. Although a majority of Vietnam veterans viewed the benefits of the experience as outweighing the costs, a vocal minority felt otherwise. Perhaps the vocal minority speak in addition for the silent minority who cannot speak: the men who gave up their lives on the battlefields of this war and who could not be represented in this study.

7

Summary and Implications

Men in the high-school class of 1963 were newly out of high school when the Vietnam era began in 1964; they were young adults when the era ended a decade later. The early years of the war were marked by heavy conscription. Because the 1.1 million men in the class were of prime draft-eligible age at this time, they served in great numbers: one-half served in the military during this era, one-fifth were sent to the Vietnam war zone. Our study sought answers to the following questions concerning the men's military experiences:

1. Who in the class of 1963 served during the Vietnam era?
2. Who did the actual fighting?
3. What was the impact of military service on veterans' later lives?
4. How did combat affect the men's later lives?
5. Did military service have different effects for different subgroups of men in the class, for example, for blacks versus whites and poor versus rich?

To answer these questions, we analyzed already-existing data from a set of tests and questionnaires that a representative sample of 1,500 of the men had filled out in 1960 and in 1974, augmented with information from a survey questionnaire designed especially for the present study, administered in 1981. The men were approximately fifteen, twenty-nine, and thirty-six years old at these three points of contact with our study. It is important to note that the study was a prospective one, encompassing information on what the men were like prior to the military service of some, as well as information on how they developed after the veterans' transition back to civilian life. Because of the availability of early, preservice information, it was possible to avoid the many pitfalls of retrospective studies and to document, more accurately than was previously possible, the antecedents as well as consequences of military service in this era and the extent to which postservice differences in the development of veterans and nonveterans were attributable to the veterans' military experience, as opposed to preexisting differences between those who served and those who did not. No other study of the Vietnam-era veteran has had this prospective, longitudinal feature. Consequently, no other study has been able to accomplish these goals in as comprehensive or accurate a manner. Figure 7–1 summarizes the answers we obtained to our questions.

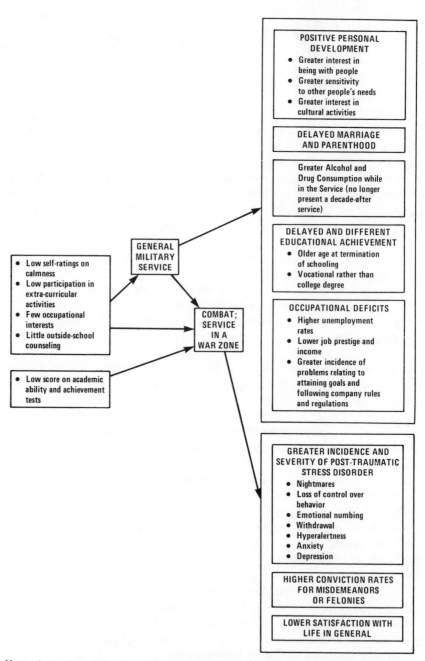

Note: Antecedents (listed on left of the diagram) were measured in the ninth grade. Consequences (listed on the right) were measured at varying points up to age thirty-six.

Figure 7–1. Overview of the Antecedents and Consequences of Military Service in the Vietnam Era for the High-School Class of 1963

Who Served?

The men who served were, on the average, similar to their classmates in terms of family background and academic abilities; however, there were psychological differences between those who served and those who did not.

The racial, socioeconomic, residential, and religious roots of the men who served were not significantly different from those of the men who did not serve. The groups' academic abilities were also similar. The draft was a factor contributing to this broad representativeness of the era force. We asked the veterans how they entered the military. Among the group of Vietnam veterans, 30 percent were drafted and served willingly, 2 percent were drafted and served unwillingly, 47 percent enlisted willingly, 15 percent enlisted unwillingly (for the sole purpose of avoiding the draft), and the remaining 5 percent felt that their entry into the military was not described by any of these four categories. Corresponding figures for non-Vietnam veterans were 21 percent, 2 percent, 51 percent, 17 percent, and 9 percent, respectively. Almost one-fifth of the veterans in the class of 1963 served against their will. The men who felt that they had been coerced into service were significantly brighter and more well-to-do than their classmates who said that they had served willingly. This implies that, without the draft, advantaged Americans would have served in fewer numbers. Opposing service patterns among black and white Americans also contributed to the overall representativeness of the force. Among blacks, the relatively brighter and richer served; the opposite was true for whites.

Although the men who did and did not serve came from similar family backgrounds, they were somewhat different in terms of their psychological profile. The men who served appeared to be less interested in or less able to manipulate their environment. While in high school, the soldiers-to-be participated in fewer extracurricular activities, expressed fewer occupational interests, received less outside-school counseling, and reported themselves to be less calm than their classmates who were later to avoid military service. One could speculate that these traits were to manifest themselves subsequently in terms of lower inclination or ability to manipulate the system and dodge the draft in an unpopular war. These conclusions are generalities that apply at the group level only. There were men spanning the entire range of backgrounds, abilities, and psychological makeup in both groups.

Who Fought?

While a broad and representative cross-section of the class served in the Vietnam era, those from disadvantaged backgrounds bore the brunt of the actual fighting of the war. For example, the army and Marine Corps carried a disproportionate share of the combat load of the Vietnam war.[1] Blacks and men from relatively poor families were overrepresented in the army and Marine Corps; whites and men from relatively well-to-do families were overrepresented in the navy, air force, and Coast Guard.[2] In addition, within the total group of men stationed in Vietnam, those of lower-than-average academic abilities reported more-frequent as well as more-intense combat experiences than those of higher-than-average abilities.

How Did Military Service Affect Men's Lives?

Military service in the Vietnam era had numerous consequences for the veterans' later lives—some positive, others negative; some transient, others long lasting and possibly permanent.[3]

Service had strong positive effects in the area of personal development. It led to greater interest in being with people, greater sensitivity to other people's needs, and greater interest in cultural activities. Both Vietnam and non-Vietnam veterans claimed that their service experiences led to deeper and more-rapid maturity on their part. Veterans also expressed appreciation for the opportunity afforded them by the service to see the world.

Military service had enormous consequences for the patterning of veterans' future life course. It led to delays in when they were able to experience critical events marking what sociologists have called the transition to adulthood: veterans finished school, got married, and became fathers at significantly older ages than their nonveteran classmates: (There is an interesting irony to this finding. Sociologically, veterans became adults at a later age than their high-school classmates. Psychologically, however, veterans became adults at an earlier age, as the previous paragraph on veterans' more-rapid maturation described.) For the most part, the impact of these sociological delays was transient. By age thirty-six, veterans had been in school the same average number of years (around thirteen) as nonveterans. Equal proportions of veterans and nonveterans (around 83 percent) were married. Veterans had relatively fewer children (under two) than nonveterans (over two), but since the men are still in their child-producing years, perhaps this difference, too, will disappear with time. The first year out of service was an especially vulnerable one for the marriages of Vietnam veterans, with over 5 percent of all Vietnam veterans' marriages (versus less than 1 percent of non-Vietnam veterans' marriages) ending in divorce in this period. By age thirty-six, however, there were no longer any significant differences between Vietnam veterans and their classmates in terms of proportions ever divorced (around one-quarter).

Also transitory were the consequences of military service for drug and alcohol use and abuse. Veterans significantly increased their intake of non-pharmacy drugs and of alcoholic beverages while they were in the service. But a decade after their exit from the service, veterans' consumption levels were no longer significantly different from those reported by their nonveteran peers.

In contrast to these fleeting consequences of the military stint for veterans' personal and family lives were the service's long-lasting consequences for veterans' educational and occupational achievements. We studied the educational and occupational development of veterans and nonveterans matched for early career potential, according to their performance in the ninth grade. Although veterans and nonveterans had attained the same number of years of schooling by age thirty-six, there were differences in the nature of the degrees received by the two groups, as well as in the distribution of the groups' educational accomplishments. Twice as many veterans as matched nonveterans (20 percent versus 10 percent) had vocational degrees; however, while only slightly more than a quarter of veterans (27 percent) were college graduates, close to a third of matched nonveterans (32 percent) were college graduates. Veterans tended to cluster around the mean of the education distribution—to have either high-school, vocational, or two-year college degrees. In contrast, the nonveteran group had significantly higher proportions of men at the bottom of the education distribution (high-school dropouts) and at the top (masters- and doctoral-degree holders). Why? Our survey data do not address this question directly, but we can speculate. Men at the bottom of the education distribution were lopped off because a disproportionately large number of high-school dropouts failed military preinduction tests. Men at the top of the education distribution were underrepresented because schooling interruptions caused by military service meant that the veterans were older than their peers when they received their postsecondary training. Veterans therefore had greater family responsibilities while in school, as well as stronger pressures to catch up with their peers. These pressures converged on the decision to seek vocational or two-year college (as opposed to four-year college) training because of the former degrees' smaller time investment and their greater payoff in terms of immediate job opportunities and starting salary. The decision had one long-lasting negative consequence, however. Veterans were steered into jobs in the secondary sector of the labor market (for example, we found that veterans were overrepresented in the mechanical and industrial trades), jobs characterized by relatively higher salaries to start but by flatter expected income curves over the life course.

Indeed, we found veterans to be behind their peers in their careers through the last point in our study (when they were thirty-six). Relative to their non-veteran classmates matched for early career potential, a greater proportion of veterans (roughly 40 percent versus 31 percent) had experienced at least one period of unemployment since leaving high school. The jobs held by veterans tended to be of slightly lower prestige and lower income (12 percent or $3,000 less in 1981). The veterans did manage to do some catching up in the decade following their exit from the military. By age thirty-six, equal proportions of Vietnam veterans, non-Vietnam veterans, and nonveterans were gainfully employed. In addition non-Vietnam veterans had caught up with their non-veteran classmates in terms of the prestige of the job they were holding. However, nonveterans were still ahead of non-Vietnam veterans in terms of income and ahead of Vietnam veterans in terms of both income and job prestige. Examination of job-prestige trends since service exit indicated that the Vietnam-veteran group would never catch up with their matched classmates on this dimension. Vietnam veterans' job-prestige curve hit its peak in 1974 and stayed stable, below the classmates' curves, after this year.

How Did Combat Affect Men's Lives?

Overlaying these consequences of general military service was a set of striking negative consequences unique to the Vietnam combat experience. These consequences were confined to Vietnam veterans' personal life and especially to their physical and psychological well-being; neither combat nor service in the Vietnam hostile-fire zone had direct effect on veterans' educational or work-related achievements.

Vietnam veterans reported a greater incidence and severity of physical problems than their classmates of similar height, weight, and general health status in the ninth grade: 23 percent of Vietnam veterans, but only 18 percent of non-Vietnam veterans and 15 percent of nonveterans, reported having a long-term health problem or disability at age thirty-six. For 11 percent of Vietnam veterans but only 8 percent of non-Vietnam veterans and 6 percent of non-veterans, this health problem was severe enough to limit their work and physical activities.

Vietnam veterans also reported a greater incidence and severity of psychological disturbances dealing with sleep-related problems, loss of control over their behavior, inability to become close to another person, withdrawal from the external environment, hyperalertness, anxiety, and depression. An indication of the magnitude of the Vietnam effect on these problems can be gleaned by comparing the proportions of Vietnam veterans, non-Vietnam veterans, and nonveterans reporting having had the following specific problems in the year preceding the 1981 survey: nightmares (21 percent, 12 percent, and 13 percent, respectively), being easily startled by a random noise (41 percent, 22 percent, 19 percent), feeling lonely (43 percent, 33 percent, 34 percent), and being unable to get emotionally close to another person (44 percent, 32 percent, 29 percent). The non-Vietnam veterans were much more similar to the nonveterans than to the Vietnam veterans in terms of the existence of these problems, leading us to conclude that the specialized Vietnam experience, not the general military-service experience, caused elevated levels of the problems. The problems, taken as a set, correspond closely to what the American Psychiatric Association has labeled posttraumatic stress disorder, lending credence to the existence of such a syndrome, as well as to its persistence over an extended time period (over a decade, in the current study).

According to our crude measuring technique, 7 percent more of the Vietnam-veteran group than of the non-Vietnam-veteran or nonveteran groups manifested symptoms associated with the disorder at age thirty-six (19 percent versus 12 percent, respectively). Group differences were presumably larger in earlier years, closer to the combat experience. Among Vietnam veterans, the incidence and severity of PTSD at midlife were not related to either the soldier's preservice characteristics or to his general adjustment to military life while in the service but were strongly related to the intensity of combat experienced as a young soldier in Vietnam. The probability of a Vietnam veteran's manifesting PTSD-related symptoms at age thirty-six increased as a function of each of the combat experiences examined in the study, experiences that took place more than a decade in the past: receiving fire from the enemy, firing one's weapon at the enemy, killing the enemy, seeing someone killed, seeing enemy wounded, seeing American wounded, seeing enemy dead, seeing American dead, being in a combat situation where survival was in jeopardy, and receiving an actual injury in the war. Among Vietnam veterans who saw heavy combat, 27 percent (more than double the baseline proportion) manifested PTSD-related symptoms at age thirty-six.

Vietnam veterans also reported slightly higher conviction rates for misdemeanors and felonies in the years following their military experience (16 percent) than did non-Vietnam veterans (13 percent) or nonveterans (9 percent). Finally, Vietnam veterans reported relatively greater dissatisfaction with the overall quality of their lives at age thirty-six than did their classmates.

Despite these long-term negative consequences of their combat experience, there was evidence that the lives of Vietnam veterans had improved since their exit from Vietnam. Their ratings of various aspects of their lives at age thirty-six—relationship with wife or girlfriend, having and raising children, occupation or job, financial security and material well-being, health, relationship with other relatives, relationship with friends, intellectual development, personal understanding and awareness, socializing and entertaining, and recreational activities—were consistently higher than similar ratings they had given in the course of a survey taken seven years prior. While this was true of their classmates' ratings too, the increases reported by Vietnam veterans tended to be greater than those reported by their classmates. In addition, Vietnam veterans' projected ratings of their lives five years into the future, when they would be forty-one years old, were more optimistic than their assessments of their present lives (albeit stilll lower than their classmates' projected ratings).

Were the Consequences Different for Different Americans?

These consequences were found for a wide cross-section of men in the class of 1963—for whites and nonwhites, for individuals of above-average and below-average socioeconomic status and of above-average and below-average academic abilities. The magnitude of the impact was roughly similar for men differing in race and ability; however, there was evidence that military service facilitiated the educational attainment of those of lower-than-average socioeconomic status to a greater extent than it did their relatively well-to-do classmates. This is not surprising when we consider the fact that one of the primary fringe benefits of service in the Vietnam era was the free schooling it offered veterans after exit from the service (the GI bill). This benefit proved to be a boon to men who would otherwise not have had the financial resources to pursue postsecondary education.

Certain service-related attitudes and behaviors exacerbated or, conversely, attenuated the consequences of military service. Relative to peers matched for social and academic advantage, educational attainment at age thirty-six was higher for veterans who served willingly, for veterans who were able to delay their service entry by at least a year after their graduation from high school, for veterans who abstained from, or consumed only moderate amounts of, alcohol while in the service, for veterans who used nonpharmacy drugs while in the service, for veterans who did not need to be formally disciplined while they were in the service, and for veterans who used the GI bill's educational benefits after leaving the service.

Among Vietnam veterans, some characteristics of the Vietnam experience were associated with later favorable evaluations of the service experience: a short duty stint inside the war zone, relatively light combat experience (specifically, not having seen Americans wounded or Vietnamese killed), officer (as opposed to enlisted-man) status, and the perception that one's unit in Vietnam was cohesive and made up of trustworthy officers and enlisted men.

There was evidence that the timing of the homecoming mediated the occupational consequences of military service. Vietnam veterans who came home in the 1970s, when antiwar sentiment was high, suffered greater occupational deficits than Vietnam veterans who came home earlier. The survey questionnaire did not tap other potentially important information relating to the homecoming—for example, did the soldier come home to a small town or a larger city, exactly what kind of reception did he receive upon return, what family and friendship networks were available to him on reentry? Therefore we do not know to what extent these aspects of the homecoming made the consequences of service different for different Americans.

Unlike another major study of the legacies of Vietnam (Kadushin, Boulanger, and Martin 1981), we found no evidence that timing of the homecoming mediated the psychological consequences of military service. The incidence of PTSD among Vietnam veterans who served early was comparable to the incidence of it among Vietnam veterans who served late, once intensity of combat was controlled. We did find lower incidence of PTSD among married Vietnam veterans and among churchgoing Vietnam veterans, but we cannot say with certainty, because of the correlational nature of our data, that these sources of support actually helped reduce postcombat emotional distress.

Optimizing the Effects of Military Service

Chance versus Choice

It is interesting to note the interplay of chance and choice, of powerlessness and efficacy, in the way events of the Vietnam era shaped these men's lives. These historical events were an often-unwelcome intrusion, interrupting the normal progress of the lives of those who served. A significant minority of the men in the class of 1963 felt, a full decade after their service experience, that they had been coerced into joining the service. Both blacks and whites were affected; although a greater percentage of black than white veterans were drafted (39 percent and 26 percent, respectively), a greater proportion of white than black veterans reported having served against their will (27 percent versus 8 percent, respectively).

Once in the service, veterans did not have the power of choice over whether they were sent to Vietnam or to other, peaceful areas of the world. Where they served made a big difference in the probable aftermath of the service experience because service in a war zone often had negative consequences that service in a peaceful area did not have. Among soldiers sent to Vietnam, there were enormous individual differences in the degree to which the men were exposed to the risks of combat. Some Vietnam veterans never experienced contact with the enemy; others found themselves often in a situation where they thought they would not survive. This element of chance made a difference in the probable impact of the service experience because development of subsequent psychological disturbances was strongly, indeed primarily, related to the severity of the combat experience. Finally, within the group of Vietnam veterans exposed to heavy combat, a small percentage of the men lost their lives while their buddies standing nearby were spared. In this instance, chance factors spelled the difference between life and death.

The men were, however, not completely at fate's mercy either. Men who managed to avoid service altogether seemed, as early as the ninth grade, to be more actively engaged in their external environment. This ability might have helped those who did not wish to serve to avoid service. In addition, certain attitudes and behaviors helped reduce men's chances of being sent to Vietnam or, once there, of being exposed to combat risks. Similarly, some strategies helped attenuate the negative aftereffects of military service. For example, enlisting, as opposed to waiting to be drafted before entering the service, was associated with reduced chances of being sent to Vietnam. Enlistment in the navy, air force, or Coast Guard (as opposed to the army or Marine Corps) was further associated with reduced chances of being exposed to heavy combat risks, given that one was sent to Vietnam. Being part of a cohesive fighting unit in which there was trust among officers and enlisted men was associated with positive evaluations of the service experience, given that one was sent to Vietnam.

Certain decisions prior to service entry, such as obtaining as much education as one could prior to entry, were associated with higher eventual educational attainment among men with similar attainment potential. Certain behaviors while in the service, such as abstention from or only moderate consumption of alcohol, and following the rules to avoid ever having to be disciplined formally, were associated with higher eventual educational attainment among men with similar attainment potential. Finally certain behaviors after leaving the service, such as making use of the GI bill, were associated with higher eventual educational attainment among men with similar attainment potential.

Overcoming Combat-Induced Psychological Problems

While development of psychological problems following heavy combat seemed to be a function of the intensity of the combat experience as opposed to preservice or in-service dispostions and behaviors, there was evidence that the existence of external social support upon return home—being married, being actively involved with a church—was associated with lower incidence of emotional distress. (We do not know the direction of cause and effect—for example, whether living alone led to heightened problems with PTSD or whether PTSD caused the family to abandon the Vietnam veteran.)

Overcoming Service-Induced Career Deficits

There was evidence that many of the negative effects of military service for later achievement were caused by life-cycle delays leading to role incompatibilities for the men. To some extent, these incompatibilities were avoidable. Figure 7-2 depicts the probable mechanism or chain of events involved. The figure suggests some strategies that could help veterans overcome the occasionally deleterious effects of service for their future work-related achievements:

1. Delay entry into the service and finish as many years of schooling as possible prior to entry.
2. While in the service, get as much training as possible in the field one eventually wants to enter.
3. Use the GI bill after the service to obtain the maximum number of years of schooling desired.
4. After military service, if additional schooling is desired, attend school full time, if possible. Do not work while in school if this impedes rapid progress toward a degree.
5. If possible, delay becoming a spouse or (especially) a parent until after one's education-related ambitions have been fulfilled.

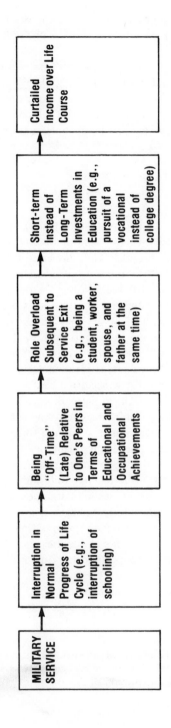

Figure 7-2. How and Why Military Service Leads to Lower Income over the Life Course for Many Veterans

6. Make long-term, as opposed to short-term, educational investments. Go to college, if that is what one really wants to do, rather than settling for a vocational license.

The men in the class of 1963 were not completely in control of the socio-political events of the 1960s that shaped their lives. But they were not at the total mercy of these events either. Knowing what one wanted and executing available behaviors to go out and get it—in short, a sense of efficacy—paid off for many of these men.

The Citizen-Soldier

The Vietnam era witnessed the decline of the concept of the citizen-soldier, the young idealist willingly giving a few years of his life in his country's service before returning to the civilian ranks. While the era force was adequately representative of America's youth in terms of its demographic composition, we found that a coercive factor—the draft—brought about this representativeness, by forcing disproportionate numbers of individuals from advantaged backgrounds to serve. We also found that the men less able or willing to avoid the draft served. As ninth graders, the soldiers-to-be showed less interest than their classmates in their school environment and in career-related matters.

Data from the present all-volunteer force indicate a continuation in these trends. Mental-aptitude scores of new accessions, especially of accessions in the army and Marine Corps, have declined since the end of the Vietnam era. The proportion of blacks in the armed forces has doubled since the start of the era. This is not to say that it is the increase in the force's minority component that has led to the decline in its academic quality level. A greater proportion of black than white enlistees in the all-volunteer force are high-school graduates (Janowitz and Moskos 1979). (This fact is important because, among enlisted men, educational qualifications in general, and possession of a high-shcool diploma in particular, have consistently emerged as the best-available predictors of military performance.) It is the underrepresentation of whites of high academic ability and of suitable educational qualifications that lies at the core of the concern about representativeness. This was true in the Vietnam era, and it remains true.

What is needed is the resurrection of the concept of the citizen-soldier. It is an old concept, one going back to the days of the founding fathers of this republic:

Safety from external danger is the most powerful director of national conduct. Even the ardent love of liberty will, after a time, give way to its dictates. The violent destruction of life and property incident to war, the continual effort and alarm attendant on a state of continual danger, will compel nations the most attached to liberty, to resort for repose and security to institutions which have a tendency to destroy their civil and political rights. To be more safe, they at length become willing to run the risk of being less free. [Hamilton 1810, p.47]

If there has to be a military, it is important that it meet the triple goals of military effectiveness, social equity, and political legitimacy (Eitelberg 1977, 1978). Vigorous reassertion of the concept of the citizen-soldier would help achieve these goals.

In closing, we note that veterans in the class of 1963 found their service experience to be worthwhile. Despite the unpopularity of the Vietnam war, exacerbated by the heavy conscription that took place, despite the psychological scars still carried by some Vietnam veterans and the attainment deficits still suffered by others, the experience was evaluated favorably by a majority of Vietnam veterans and non-Vietnam veterans in the class. There were exceptions, of course, but overall, the experience's positive impact on personal growth and maturation was seen as overriding.

Notes

1. Ninety-two percent of Vietnam veterans in these two service branches (versus only 65 percent of Vietnam veterans in the navy, air force, and Coast Guard) reported receiving fire from the enemy, 69 percent (versus 35 percent) reported firing their weapon at the enemy, 46 percent (versus 21 percent) reported killing the enemy, 69 percent (versus 48 percent) reported seeing someone get killed, 70 percent (versus 38 percent) reported seeing enemy wounded, 89 percent (versus 67 percent) reported seeing American wounded, 77 percent (versus 39 percent) reported seeing enemy dead, 78 percent (versus 60 percent) reported seeing American dead, and 74 percent (versus 45 percent) reported finding themselves in a combat situation where they thought they would not survive.

2. Thirteen percent of the former branches but only 7 percent of the latter were nonwhite; 60 percent of the former branches but only 50 percent of the latter were of lower-than-average socioeconomic status.

3. We weighted the 1981 survey data so that our groups of Vietnam veterans, non-Vietnam veterans, and nonveterans were matched in terms of fifty-one preservice characteristics measured when the men were about fifteen years old. The purpose of this group-matching procedure was to ensure that, to the maximum extent possible, postservice differences among the three groups could rightfully be attributed to the military experiences of the veterans, as opposed to the preexisting differences between those who served and fought and those who did not. All findings reported under questions 3, 4, and 5 are from the matched samples.

References

Abeles, Ronald P., and Wise, Lauress L. Coping with attrition in a longitudinal study: The case of Project TALENT. *Journal of Economics and Business,* 1979-1980, *32,* 170-181.

American Psychiatric Association Task Force on Nomenclature and Statistics. *Diagnostic and Statistical Manual of Mental Disorders (Third Edition).* Washington, D.C.: American Psychiatric Press, Inc., 1980.

Barret-Ruger, Drue, and Lammers, Craig A. Vietnam combat veterans: Assessment of pre-military and military influences on post-military adjustment. Paper presented at the American Psychological Association Convention, Los Angeles, 1981.

Bonds, Ray. *The Vietnam War.* New York: Crown Publishers, 1979.

Borus, J.F. Incidence of maladjustment in Vietnam returnees. *Archives of General Psychiatry,* 1974, *30,* 554-557.

Card, J.J., Goodstadt, B.E.; Gross, D.E.; and Shanner, W.M. *Development of a ROTC/Army Career Commitment Model.* Palo Alto: American Institutes for Research, 1975.

Card, Josefina Jayme; Steel, Lauri; and Abeles, Ronald P. Sex differences in realization of individual potential for achievement. *Journal of Vocational Behavior,* 1980, *17,* 1-21.

Carr, R.A. *A comparison of self-concept and expectations concerning control between Vietnam-era veterans and non-veterans.* Ph.D. dissertation, St. Louis University, 1973.

Dean, D.G. Alienation: Its meaning and measurement. *American Sociological Review,* 1961, *26,* 753-758.

DeFazio, V.J. The Vietnam era veteran: Psychological problems. *Journal of Contemporary Psychotherapy,* 1975, *7,* 9-15.

Derogatis, Leonard R.; Rickels, Karl; and Rock, Anthony F. The SCL-90 and the MMPI: A step in the validation of a new self-report scale. *British Journal of Psychiatry,* 1976, *128,* 280-289.

Derogatis, Leonard R., and Cleary, Patricia A. Confirmation of the dimensional structure of the SCL-90: A study in construct validation. *Journal of Clinical Psychology,* 1977, *33,* 981-989.

Diagnostic and Statistical Manual, Edition I. Washington, D.C.: American Psychiatric Association, 1952.

Diagnostic and Statistical Manual, Edition II. Washington, D.C.: American Psychiatric Association, 1968.

Diagnostic and Statistical Manual, Edition III. Washington, D.C.: American Psychiatric Association, 1980.

Egendorf, Arthur; Kadushin, Charles; Laufer, Robert S.; Rothbart, George; and Sloan, Lee. *Summary of Findings.* Volume I of *Legacies of Vietnam:*

Comparative Adjustment of Veterans and their Peers. Washington, D.C.:
   U.S. Government Printing Office, 1981.

Eitelberg, Mark J. *Evaluation of Army Representation,* TR-77-A9. Alexandria,
   Va.: U.S. Army Research Institute for the Behavioral and Social Sciences,
   1977.

Eitelberg, Mark J. American youth and military representation: In search of
   the perfect portrait. *Youth and Society,* 1978, *10*(1), 5-31.

Enzie, R.R., Sawyer, R.N., and Montgomery, F.A. Manifest anxiety of Vietnam
   returnees and undergraduates. *Psychological Reports,* 1973, *33,* 446.

Figley, Charles R., ed. *Stress Disorders among Vietnam Veterans.* New York:
   Brunner/Mazel, 1978a.

Figley, Charles R. Symptoms of delayed combat stress among a college sample
   of Vietnam veterans. *Military Medicine,* 1978b, *143,* 107-110.

Figley, Charles R., and Stretch, Robert H. *Vietnam veterans questionnaire.*
   Paper prepared for the Veterans Administration under contract V101
   (134C)P-693. January 1980. (Available from C.R. Figley, Family Research
   Institute, Purdue University, West Lafayette, Indiana.)

Figley, Charles R. Personal communication to William S. Farrell, July 2, 1980.

Figley, C.R., and Eisenhart, W. Contrasts between combat and non-combat
   Vietnam veterans regarding selected indices of interpersonal adjustment.
   Paper presented at the annual meeting of the American Sociological
   Association, San Francisco, August 1975.

Flanagan, John C., and Russ-Eft, Darlene. *An Empirical Study to Aid in Formu-
   lating Educational Goals.* Palo Alto: American Institutes for Research,
   1975.

Fligstein, Neil D. Who served in the military: 1940-73. *Armed Forces and
   Society,* 1980, *6,* 297-312.

Ginzberg, Eli. *The Ineffective Soldier: Lessons for Management and the Nation.*
   Westport, Conn.: Greenwood Press, 1975.

Hamilton, A. (1788). The Federalist, Number VIII, in *The Works of Alexander
   Hamilton.* New York: Williams & Whiting, 1810.

Helzer, J.E.; Robins, L.N.; and Davis, D.H. Depressive disorders in Vietnam
   returnees. *Journal of Nervous and Mental Disease,* 1976, *163,* 177-185.

Hodge, R.W., Siegel, P.M.; and Rossi, P.H. Occupational prestige in the United
   States: 1925-63. *American Journal of Sociology,* 1964, *70,* 286-302.

Hogan, Dennis P. *Transitions and Social Change.* New York: Academic Press,
   1981.

Janowitz, Morris, and Moskos, Charles C. Jr. Five years of the all-volunteer
   force: 1973-1978. *Armed Forces and Society,* 1979, *5,* 171-218.

Kadushin, Charles; Boulanger, Ghislaine; and Martin, John. *Long-term Stress
   Reactions: Some Causes, Consequences, and Naturally Occurring Support
   Systems.* Volume 4 of *Legacies of Vietnam: Comparative Adjustment of
   Veterans and Their Peers.* Washington, D.C.: U.S. Government Printing
   Office, 1981.

King, Allan G. Is occupational segregation the cause of the flatter experience-earnings profiles of women? *Journal of Human Resources,* 1977, *12,* 541-549.

Laufer, Robert S.; Yager, Thomas; Frey-Wouters, Ellen; Donnellan, Joan; Gallops, Mark; and Stenbeck, Kathy. *Post-War Trauma: Social and Psychological Problems of Vietnam Veterans in the Aftermath of the Vietnam War.* Volume 3 of *Legacies of Vietnam: Comparative Adjustment of Veterans and Their Peers.* Washington, D.C.: U.S. Government Printing Office, 1981.

McDermott, Walter F. The influence of Vietnam combat on subsequent psychopathology. Paper presented at the American Psychological Association Convention, Los Angeles, 1981.

Moskos, Charles C., Jr. The American dilemma in uniform: Race in the armed forces. *Annals of the American Academy of Political and Social Science,* 1973, *406,* 94-106.

Neal, Arthur G., and Groat, H. Theodore. Social class correlates of stability and change in levels of alienation: A longitudinal study. *Sociological Quarterly,* 1974, *15,* 548-558.

Newsweek. Viet vets fight back. November 12, 1979, pp. 44, 49.

Penk, W.E.; Robinowitz, R.; Roberts, R.; Patterson, E.T.; Dolan, M.P.; and Atkins, H.G. Adjustment differences among male substance abusers varying in degree of combat experience in Vietnam. *Journal of Consulting and Clinical Psychology,* 1981, *49,* 426-436.

Rosenfeld, Rachel A. Women's employment patterns and occupational achievements. *Social Science Research,* 1978, *7,* 61-80.

Rothbart, George; Sloan, Lee; and Joyce, Kathleen. *Educational and Work Careers: Men in the Vietnam Generation.* Volume 2 of *Legacies of Vietnam: Comparative Adjustment of Veterans and Their Peers.* Washington, D.C.: U.S. Government Printing Office, 1981.

Sorensen, A.B., and Tuma, Nancy Brandon. Labor market structures and job mobility. *Research in Social Stratification and Mobility,* 1981, *1,* 67-94.

Spilerman, Seymour. Careers, labor market structure, and socioeconomic achievement. *American Journal of Sociology,* 1977, *83,* 551-593.

Stampler, Frederick M., and Sipprelle, R. Carl. The psychological adjustment of Vietnam era veterans: The next decade. Paper presented at the American Psychological Association Convention, Los Angeles, 1981.

Stouffer, Samuel A.; Suchman, Edward A.; DeVinney, Leland C.; Starr, Shirley A.; and Williams, Robin M., Jr. *The American Soldier (Volumes 1 and 2).* Princeton, N.J.: Princeton University Press, 1949.

Strange, R.E. Psychiatric perspectives of the Vietnam veteran. *Military Medicine,* 1974, *139,* 96-98.

Strayer, Richard, and Ellenhorn, Lewis. Vietnam veterans: A study exploring adjustment patterns and attitudes. *Journal of Social Issues,* 1975, *31*(4), 81-91.

Suter, Larry E., and Miller, Herman P. Income differences between men and career women. *American Journal of Sociology,* 1973, *78,* 962–974.

U.S. Veterans Administration. *Data on Vietnam Era Veterans, September 1979.* Washington, D.C.: Reports and Statistics Service, Office of the Controller, Veterans Administration, 1979.

U.S. Veterans Administration. *Veterans Benefits under Current Educational Programs.* Washington, D.C.: Veterans Administration, Office of the Controller, Reports and Statistics Service, March 1980.

Wise, Lauress L. The fight against attrition in longitudinal research. Paper presented at the American Educational Research Association, New York, April 4–8, 1977.

Wise, Lauress L.; McLaughlin, Donald H.; and Steel, Lauri. *The Project TALENT Data Bank Handbook.* Palo Alto: American Institutes for Research, 1979.

Worthington, E.R. Post-service adjustment and Vietnam era veterans. *Military Medicine,* 1977, *142,* 865–866.

Worthington, E.R. Demographic and pre-service variables as predictors of post-military service adjustment. In Figley, Charles R, ed. *Stress Disorders among Vietnam Veterans.* New York: Brunner/Mazel, 1978.

Appendix:
The 1981 Survey
Questionnaire

General Instructions

This questionnaire contains two kinds of questions:

1. Fill in the blank.
2. Multiple choice.

For the first kind of question, just write the information requested in the space provided. Example:

When were you born?

<u> June / 10 / 1945 </u>
    month   day   year

For the second kind of question, circle the number next to the answer you have chosen. Circle only one answer for each question, unless specified otherwise. Examples:

What is your current marital status?

1. Never married
2. Married
③ Separated
4. Divorced or annulled
5. Widowed

Which of the following people live with you in the same household?

		Yes	No
a.	Wife or girlfriend	1	②
b.	Children	①	2
c.	Other relatives	1	②
d.	Other people not related to you	1	②

Group Classification Question

This study involves three groups of Project TALENT participants, all of whom were in the ninth grade in 1960. We want to make sure that you are classified in the correct group. To which group do you belong (*circle one*):

1. Veterans who served in Vietnam—Men who served/are serving on active military duty (Army, Navy, Air Force, Marine Corps, or Coast Guard) *and* who once served in the Vietnam hostile fire zone.
2. Veterans who never served in Vietnam—Men who served/are serving on active military duty (Army, Navy, Air Force, Marine Corps, or Coast Guard) who *never* served in the Vietnam hostile fire zone.
3. Nonveterans—Men who never served on active military duty.

Section I. Background

This first set of questions deals with your living situation, education, employment, and marital history. Please mark your answers in the blanks provided. For multiple choice questions, please circle only one answer for each question, unless specified otherwise.

A. When were you born?   _____ / _____ / _____
                          month   day   year

B. Where do you live?   _____ / _____ / _____
                          city or town state or country zip code

C. What is the size of this community? (Circle one number corresponding to your answer.)
    1. Rural
    2. Small town or city (under 20,000 population; not rural)
    3. Medium-sized town or city (20,000–249,999)
    4. Large city (250,000–1,499,999)
    5. Very large city (over 1,500,000)
D. How many years have you lived in this city or town?_____ year(s).
E. In how many different communities (towns, cities, or military bases) have you lived since 1960?_____ different towns, cities, or military bases.
F. Which of the following are you? (Circle all that apply.)
    1. White/Caucasian
    2. Black/Negro/Afro-American
    3. Mexican-American/Chicano
    4. Oriental
    5. American Indian
    6. Puerto Rican-American
    7. Other (please specify:_____)

G. Do you consider yourself to be:
1. Protestant
2. Catholic
3. Jewish
4. Other religion (please specify: _____)
5. Unaffiliated with any religion

H. Which of the following people live with you in the same household?

	Yes	No
H-a. Wife or girlfriend	1	2
H-b. Children	1	2
H-c. Other relatives	1	2
H-d. Other people not related to you	1	2

I. What is your current marital status?
1. Never married
2. Married
3. Separated
4. Divorced or annulled
5. Widowed

If you have never been married, skip to question L.

J. Please list the date(s) of your marriage(s) and any separations, divorces, and/or deaths.

	Date of Marriage	Date of Separation from Wife	Date of Divorce	Date of Death of Wife
J-a. First marriage	___/___ month year	___/___ month year	___/___ month year	___/___ month year
J-b. Second marriage	___/___ month year	___/___ month year	___/___ month year	___/___ month year
J-c. Third marriage	___/___ month year	___/___ month year	___/___ month year	___/___ month year
J-d. Fourth marriage	___/___ month year	___/___ month year	___/___ month year	___/___ month year
J-e. Fifth marriage	___/___ month year	___/___ month year	___/___ month year	___/___ month year

K. How many children do you have? (Write in the numbers, including 0 if you have none.)
K-a. Natural children _____
K-b. Adopted children, stepchildren, or foster children _____

L. Please circle *one* number on the scale below indicating how many years of formal education you have completed.

Elementary	*High School*	*College*	*Postcollege*
1 2 3 4 5 6 7 8	9 10 11 12	13 14 15 16	17 or more

M. Please indicate which of the following diplomas or degrees you have obtained and the year in which you received the degree.

	Have you received this degree?		If yes, when?
	Yes	*No*	
M-a. High-school diploma or GED	1	2	19 ____
M-b. Vocational-training certificate	1	2	19 ____
M-c. 2-year or junior-college degree (A.A.)	1	2	19 ____
M-d. 4-year college degree (B.A. or B.S.)	1	2	19 ____
M-e. Masters degree (M.A. or M.S.)	1	2	19 ____
M-f. Doctorate or equivalent (Ph.D., M.D., etc.)	1	2	19 ____

N. Did you use the GI bill to help finance your education?
1. Yes
2. No

O. Which of the following best describes your current employment situation? (Circle one.)
1. Working full time.
2. Working part time, looking for full-time work.
3. Working part time, not looking for full-time work.
4. Not working, but looking for work.
5. Not working, not looking for work.
6. Not working, unable to work (poor health, attending school, etc.).

If you are not working, skip to question X.

Questions P through W are for working respondents only. If you are working at more than one job, answer the questions in terms of what you consider to be your principal or primary job.

P. Which of the following are you?
1. An employee of a private company, business, or individual for wages, salary, or commissions.
2. A government employee (federal, state, county, or local government).

3. Self-employed in own business, professional practice, or farm.
4. Working without pay in a family business or farm.
5. Working for pay in a family business or farm.
6. Other.

Q. What is your job title? _____

R. What kind of business is this (for example, junior high school, auto-assembly plant, retail supermarket, etc.)? _____

S. Briefly, what do you do on your job? Please be specific. _____
_____

T. What is the usual number of hours you spend per week working on this job? _____ hours per week.

U. Approximately how much is your pay on this job, before taxes and deductions? (Fill in any one blank.)
$____ per hour or $____ per week or $____ per month or $____ per year

V. In your view, how satisfied is your employer with your work performance?
1. Extremely satisfied
2. Very satisfied
3. Satisfied
4. Not too satisfied
5. Not at all satisfied
6. I am self-employed and have no employer

W. Are any of the following a problem for you in your current job?

	Not a problem	Somewhat of a problem	A large problem
W-a. Getting along with supervisors	1	2	3
W-b. Getting along with other workers	1	2	3
W-c. Coping with deadlines and time pressures	1	2	3
W-d. Being late or absent from work	1	2	3
W-e. Following company rules and regulations	1	2	3
W-f. Your salary	1	2	3
W-g. Attaining goals you set for yourself	1	2	3

X. How many full-time jobs have you had since 1960? (Do not include summer jobs.) _____ full-time jobs.

Y. Please describe these full-time jobs in terms of what you were doing, for whom, and when.

Job Number	Job Title and Kind of Business	Date Started Job (Mo. & Yr.)	Date Ended Job (Mo. & Yr.)
Y-a. 1st full-time job		/ mo. yr.	/ mo. yr.
Y-b. 2nd full-time job		/ mo. yr.	/ mo. yr.
Y-c. 3rd full-time job		/ mo. yr.	/ mo. yr.
Y-d. 4th full-time job		/ mo. yr.	/ mo. yr.
Y-e. 5th full-time job		/ mo. yr.	/ mo. yr.
Y-f. 6th full-time job		/ mo. yr.	/ mo. yr.
Y-g. 7th full-time job		/ mo. yr.	/ mo. yr.
Y-h. 8th full-time job		/ mo. yr.	/ mo. yr.
Y-i. 9th full-time job		/ mo. yr.	/ mo. yr.
Y-j. 10th full-time job		/ mo. yr.	/ mo. yr.

Z.   Since 1960, how many periods of unemployment have you had (periods lasting over a month when you were not working but looking for work)? _____ periods of unemployment.

AA.   Please give us the dates of these periods of unemployment.

Unemployment Period Number	Date Unemployment Started (Mo. & Yr.)	Date Unemployment Ended (Mo. & Yr.)
AA-a. 1st period	/ month year	/ month year
AA-b. 2nd period	/ month year	/ month year
AA-c. 3rd period	/ month year	/ month year
AA-d. 4th period	/ month year	/ month year
AA-e. 5th period	/ month year	/ month year

Unemployment Period Number	Date Unemployment Started (Mo. & Yr.)	Date Unemployment Ended (Mo. & Yr.)
AA-f. 6th period	_____/_____ month year	_____/_____ month year
AA-g. 7th period	_____/_____ month year	_____/_____ month year
AA-h. 8th period	_____/_____ month year	_____/_____ month year
AA-i. 9th period	_____/_____ month year	_____/_____ month year
AA-j. 10th period	_____/_____ month year	_____/_____ month year

BB. What was your household's (self plus spouse) gross income in 1979? (If you have trouble remembering, this would be the same as reported on your 1979 federal income tax form.)
1. Under $5,000
2. $5,000 to $9,999
3. $10,000 to $14,999
4. $15,000 to $19,999
5. $20,000 to $24,999
6. $25,000 to $29,999
7. $30,000 to $34,999
8. $35,000 to $39,999
9. $40,000 or over

CC. Are you receiving or have you received military disability or pension payments?
1. Yes
2. No

DD. Do you own your own home?
1. Yes, I bought it with the help of the GI bill or another veterans' program.
2. Yes, I bought it without the help of the GI bill or veterans' assistance.
3. No.

EE. Have you ever had trouble getting or keeping credit?
1. Yes, more than once.
2. Yes, once.
3. No, never.

FF. Do you ever run out of money before you have paid all your monthly bills (rent, house payment, utilities, car payment, loan payment, credit card payments, etc.)?

1. Yes, frequently.
2. Yes, once in a while.
3. No.

GG. How much money do you have in savings or investments (not counting the value of your home)?
   1. None
   2. Less than one month's household income
   3. One to three months' household income
   4. Three months' to one year's household income
   5. More than one year's household income

Section II. Health

This section of the questionnaire deals with your health and health-related activities.

A. Which of the following best describes your usual health in the last 3 years?
   1. Very good
   2. Good
   3. Fair
   4. Poor
   5. Very poor
B. Do you have a long-term health problem or a disability?
   1. Yes, military related
   2. Yes, but not military related
   3. No (Skip to item F)
C. If you answered yes to B, please describe this long-term health problem or disability.

   _____

   _____

D. If you answered yes to B, does this long-term health problem or disability limit the kind or amount of work or activity you can do?
   1. Yes
   2. No
E. If you answered yes to B, are you currently taking medication for this long-term health problem or disability?
   1. Yes
   2. No
F. How many packs of cigarettes do you smoke a day?
   1. None
   2. Less than half a pack
   3. Between half a pack and a pack

4. One to two packs
5. More than two packs

G. How often do you drink at least one six-pack of beer, or a bottle of wine, or five drinks of liquor in one day?
1. Never
2. Rarely
3. Once or twice a month
4. Once a week
5. Several times a week
6. Almost every day

H. How many days of illness have you had during the past year (that is, days in which you missed work or other activities)?
1. None
2. One to two days
3. Three to seven days
4. Eight to fourteen days
5. Fifteen to thirty days
6. More than thirty days

I. How often do you use the following mediations or drugs?

	Daily	Several times a week	Several times a month	Every few months	Rarely or never
I-a. Pain medication (asprin, Tylenol, Darvon, etc.)	1	2	3	4	5
I-b. Tranquilizers (Valium, Librium, etc.)	1	2	3	4	5
I-c. Sedatives or sleeping pills (Sleep-eez, barbiturates, etc.)	1	2	3	4	5
I-d. Prescription stimulants (Dexedrine, diet pills, etc.)	1	2	3	4	5
I-e. Other stimulants (No-Doz, Vivarin, etc.)	1	2	3	4	5
I-f. Narcotics (codeine, morphine)	1	2	3	4	5
I-g. Other drugs (including marijuana and street drugs)	1	2	3	4	5

J. During the past fifteen years, have you sought help or counseling for a problem in any of the following areas?

	No	Yes, once	Yes, more than once
J-a. Marital, family, or job-related adjustment	1	2	3
J-b. Alcohol or drug use	1	2	3
J-c. Nervous condition	1	2	3
J-d. Other mental health problem	1	2	3

K. During the past fifteen years, have you been hospitalized for a problem in any of these areas?

	No	Yes, once	Yes, more than once
K-a. Marital, family, or job-related adjustment	1	2	3
K-b. Alcohol or drug use	1	2	3
K-c. Nervous condition	1	2	3
K-d. Other mental health problem	1	2	3

L. How often during the past year—

	Daily	Several times a week	Several times a month	Every few months	Rarely or never
L-a. Have you had difficulty sleeping?	1	2	3	4	5
L-b. Has your sleep been disturbed during the night by troubling thoughts?	1	2	3	4	5
L-c. Have you had nightmares?	1	2	3	4	5
L-d. Have you had serious difficulty getting up in the morning?	1	2	3	4	5

M. If you circled 1, 2, or 3 to items L-a, b, c, or d above, in what year did your sleep-related problem(s) start? (Make an estimate even if you are unsure.) In 19_____.

Section III. Quality of Life

This section of the survey is concerned with your feelings about the general quality of your life.

A. Please rate your overall satisfaction in each of the following categories. Circle one answer for each category.

			Satisfaction		
		Very Low	Low	Moderate	High	Very High
A-a.	Relationship with wife or girlfriend	1	2	3	4	5
A-b.	Having and raising children	1	2	3	4	5
A-c.	Occupation	1	2	3	4	5
A-d.	Financial security and material well-being	1	2	3	4	5
A-e.	Health	1	2	3	4	5
A-f.	Relationship with other relatives	1	2	3	4	5
A-g.	Relationship with friends	1	2	3	4	5
A-h.	Intellectual development	1	2	3	4	5
A-i.	Personal understanding and awareness	1	2	3	4	5
A-j.	Socializing and entertaining	1	2	3	4	5
A-k.	Recreational activities	1	2	3	4	5

B. Suppose we say that on the scales below, 1 represents the worst possible life for you and 10 represents the best possible life for you.

B-a. Where would you put your present life? (circle one number.)

Worst   Best
Possible   Possible
Life   Life

1   2   3   4   5   6   7   8   9   10

B-b. Where would you put your life as you think it will be five years from now?

Worst   Best
Possible   Possible
Life   Life

1   2   3   4   5   6   7   8   9   10

C. Please indicate the extent to which you agree or disagree with each of the following statements.

		Agree strongly	Agree mildly	Disagree mildly	Disagree strongly
C-a.	Sometimes I feel all alone in the world.	1	2	3	4

		Agree strongly	Agree mildly	Disagree mildly	Disagree strongly
C-b.	There are few dependable ties between people any more.	1	2	3	4
C-c.	People are just naturally considerate and helpful.	1	2	3	4
C-d.	The world we live in is basically a friendly place.	1	2	3	4
C-e.	Most people are not really sincere in their relations with others.	1	2	3	4
C-f.	The way things are now, a person has to look out pretty much for himself.	1	2	3	4
C-g.	Most married people in our country lead trapped and frustrated lives.	1	2	3	4
C-h.	Real friends are as easy to find as ever.	1	2	3	4
C-i.	Most people seldem feel lonely.	1	2	3	4

D. People sometimes have problems in their lives. Please consider each area below and rate the extent to which it has been a problem for you during the past year. Then (for those who served on active duty in the military) tell us whether the problems you marked as "minor" or "serious" were caused or made worse by your military experience.

		Has this been a problem?			Military related?	
		Not a problem	A minor problem	A serious problem	Yes	No
D-a.	Getting along with my wife or girlfriend	1	2	3	1	2
D-b.	Getting along with friends and neighbors	1	2	3	1	2
D-c.	Getting along with my family	1	2	3	1	2
D-d.	Having someone I can be emotionally close to	1	2	3	1	2
D-e.	Enjoying sex	1	2	3	1	2

		Has this been a problem?			Military related?	
		Not a problem	*A minor problem*	*A serious problem*	*Yes*	*No*
D-f.	Enjoying free time and recreation	1	2	3	1	2
D-g.	Getting on track in my life	1	2	3	1	2

E. Below is a list of things that sometimes bother people. For each item in the list please indicate how much it has distressed or bothered you during the past year. Then (for those who served on active duty in the military), tell us whether the problems causing you "somewhat" or "quite a bit" of distress were caused or made worse by your military experience.

		How much has this distressed you?			Military related?	
		Not at all	*Somewhat*	*Quite a bit*	*Yes*	*No*
E-a.	Feeling restless or jittery	1	2	3	1	2
E-b.	Arguing a lot	1	2	3	1	2
E-c.	Feeling that nobody cares about you	1	2	3	1	2
E-d.	Letting little things anger you	1	2	3	1	2
E-e.	Being unable to get excited about things	1	2	3	1	2
E-f.	Wanting to hurt people	1	2	3	1	2
E-g.	Feeling that life isn't worth living	1	2	3	1	2
E-h.	Feelings of loneliness	1	2	3	1	2
E-i.	Wanting to break or destroy something	1	2	3	1	2
E-j.	Feeling nervous	1	2	3	1	2
E-k.	Feeling apprehensive or fearful for no apparent reason	1	2	3	1	2
E-l.	Knowing that you can't control your temper	1	2	3	1	2
E-m.	Feeling tense	1	2	3	1	2
E-n.	Feeling that things won't be any better tomorrow	1	2	3	1	2
E-o.	Being easily startled by random noises	1	2	3	1	2

F. How many traffic-related tickets have you had since 1960 (do not count parking tickets)?
   1. None
   2. 1–2
   3. 3–5
   4. 6–10
   5. 11–15
   6. More than 15
G. Have you ever been arrested since 1960?
   1. No
   2. Yes, once
   3. Yes, more than once
H. Have you ever been convicted of a misdemeanor or felony since 1960?
   1. No
   2. Yes, once
   3. Yes, more than once
I. Following is a list of traits that have been shown to vary from person to person. How would you rate yourself on each trait, in comparison to other American men of your age?

	Much less than others	Somewhat less than others	About the same as others	Somewhat more than others	Much more than others
I-a. Interest in being with people	1	2	3	4	5
I-b. Sensitivity to other people's needs	1	2	3	4	5
I-c. Impulsiveness	1	2	3	4	5
I-d. Energy	1	2	3	4	5
I-e. Calmness	1	2	3	4	5
I-f. Tidiness, neatness	1	2	3	4	5
I-g. Interest in cultural activities	1	2	3	4	5
I-h. Leadership capacity	1	2	3	4	5
I-i. Self-confidence	1	2	3	4	5
I-j. Maturity	1	2	3	4	5
I-k. Self-reliance	1	2	3	4	5
I-l. Capacity to tolerate stress	1	2	3	4	5
I-m. Capacity to adapt to change	1	2	3	4	5

J. How active are you in each of the following kinds of organizations? (Circle the highest number that applies in each row.)

	Not a member	A member but rarely participate	Participate occasionally	Spend time each month with this organization	Active in the leadership
J-a. Church	1	2	3	4	5
J-b. Social organizations (e.g., swim and tennis clubs)	1	2	3	4	5
J-c. Civic organizations (e.g., political parties, community or boards)	1	2	3	4	5
J-d. Professional organizations (including unions)	1	2	3	4	5
J-e. Charitable organizations (e.g., Lions Club, Kiwanis, Rotary)	1	2	3	4	5

For those who never served on active duty in the military:

K. Which one of the following best describes your nonparticipation in the military?
    1. I was willing to serve, but I was not drafted.
    2. I was not willing to serve, and I was not drafted.
    3. I was not willing to serve, and I took steps to avoid being drafted.
    4. Other. (Please explain): _____

_____

You are done! Thank you for your cooperation!

For military veterans or active military personnel:

L. Which one of the following best describes your entry into the military?
    1. I was drafted, and I served willingly.
    2. I was drafted, and I served unwillingly.
    3. I enlisted, willingly.
    4. I enlisted, unwillingly (for example, to avoid the draft).
    5. Other. (Please explain): _____

_____

Please continue with section IV concerning your military experience.

Section IV. Military Service

A. For each of the following branches of the military in which you have served,
    please fill in your dates of service.

    A-a. Army-active duty   from   ___/___ to ___/___
                                                        mo. yr.   mo. yr.

    A-b. Navy-active duty   from   ___/___ to ___/___
                                                        mo. yr.   mo. yr.

    A-c. Air Force-active duty   from   ___/___ to ___/___
                                                        mo. yr.   mo. yr.

    A-d. Marine Corps-active duty   from   ___/___ to ___/___
                                                       mo. yr.   mo. yr.

    A-e. Coast Guard-active duty   from   ___/___ to ___/___
                                                       mo. yr.   mo. yr.

The next several questions deal with your experiences in the military. If you
served in more than one branch of the military, answer the questions as they
relate to your primary service branch, that is, the one in which you performed
active duty or spent the longest period of time.

B. At what rank did you enter the service? _____
C. What is the highest rank you achieved while on active duty in the service?
    _____
D. What is the highest rank you achieved while in the Reserves?_____
E. Have you received any personal decorations for combat or outstanding
    service? (Do not count unit or "automatic" decorations.)
        1. Yes. How many? _____
        2. No.
F. How many times did you receive disciplinary action while in the service,
    such as being demoted, getting busted, or put in the stockade?
        1. Never
        2. 1 or 2 times
        3. 3 or 4 times
        4. 5 times or more
G. What kind of discharge did you receive from the service?
        1. Honorable
        2. General
        3. Undesirable
        4. Bad conduct
        5. Dishonorable
        6. Medical
        7. Does not apply; I am still in the service

H. How often did you drink at least one six-pack of beer, or a bottle of wine, or five drinks of liquor in one day—

H-a. before entering the service?
1. Never
2. Rarely
3. Once or twice a month
4. Once a week
5. Several times a week
6. Almost every day

H-b. while in the service?
1. Never
2. Rarely
3. Once or twice a month
4. Once a week
5. Several times a week
6. Almost every day

I. How often did you use drugs (other than pharmacy drugs for a physical ailment)—

I-a. before entering the service?
1. Never
2. Rarely
3. Once or twice a month
4. Once a week
5. Several times a week
6. Almost every day

I-b. while in the service?
1. Never
2. Rarely
3. Once or twice a month
4. Once a week
5. Several times a week
6. Almost every day

J. What effect has military service had on your life?
1. Entirely positive effects
2. Mostly positive effects
3. An equal balance of positive and negative effects
4. Mostly negative effects
5. Entirely negative effects.

K. Please explain briefly, in your own words, your answer to J above.

_____

_____

_____

_____

L. Did you serve in any of the following locations while in the military?

		Yes	No
L-a.	Vietnam or near Vietnam where you were exposed to hostile fire	1	2
L-b.	Asia, other than Vietnam	1	2
L-c.	United States	1	2
L-d.	Europe	1	2
L-e.	Middle East	1	2
L-f.	Other. Please specify: _____		

If you served in Vietnam (or near Vietnam in the hostile-fire zone) please answer
the last eleven questions below. If you never served in the Vietnam fire zone,
you are done filling out the questionnaire. Thank you for your cooperation.

M. How long did you serve in or around Vietnam?
1. Less than 1 month
2. 1–3 months
3. 4–6 months
4. 7–9 months
5. 10–12 months
6. More than 12 months

Vietnam Service Dates
First Tour
from _____ / _____ to _____ / _____
month year   month year
Second Tour (if applicable)
from _____ / _____ to _____ / _____
month year   month year

N. During your Vietnam service were you:
1. A commissioned officer
2. A noncommissioned officer
3. An enlisted man

O. While in the Vietnam arena, how often (if ever) did you:

	Very Often	Often	Occasionally	Rarely, but at least once	Never
O-a. Receive fire from the enemy?	1	2	3	4	5
O-b. Fire your weapon at the enemy?	1	2	3	4	5
O-c. Kill the enemy?	1	2	3	4	5
O-d. See someone get killed?	1	2	3	4	5
O-e. See enemy wounded?	1	2	3	4	5
O-f. See American wounded?	1	2	3	4	5

	Very Often	Often	Occasionally	Rarely, but at least once	Never
O-g. See enemy dead?	1	2	3	4	5
O-h. See American dead?	1	2	3	4	5
O-i. Find yourself in a combat situation where you thought you might not survive?	1	2	3	4	5

P. Were you injured in the Vietnam war?
   1. Yes; with an injury requiring hospitalization.
   2. Yes, with an injury not requiring hospitalization.
   3. No.

Q. Please describe your primary duties while serving in the Vietnam arena.

_____

_____

_____

R. Did you train with most of the men in your unit?
   1. Yes
   2. No

S. How cohesive was the unit you served with in Vietnam?
   1. We were extremely close.
   2. We were very close.
   3. We were fairly close.
   4. We were not very close.
   5. We were not close at all.

T. How much did you trust the commissioned officers you served with in Vietnam?
   1. I trusted them completely.
   2. I trusted them a great deal.
   3. I trusted them somewhat.
   4. I didn't trust them very much.
   5. I didn't trust them at all.

U. How much did you trust the noncommissioned officers you served with in Vietnam?
   1. I trusted them completely.
   2. I trusted them a great deal.
   3. I trusted them somewhat.
   4. I didn't trust them very much.
   5. I didn't trust them at all.

V. How much did you trust the enlisted men you served with in Vietnam?
    1. I trusted them completely.
    2. I trusted them a great deal.
    3. I trusted them somewhat.
    4. I didn't trust them very much.
    5. I didn't trust them at all.
W. Please tell us briefly, in your own words, how your experiences in Vietnam
    have affected your life.

    _____
    _____
    _____
    _____

You are done! Thank you for your cooperation!

Please check your answers and then return the completed questionnaire in the
enclosed postage-paid envelope.

Index

About the Author

Josefina J. Card is a principal research scientist at the American Institutes for Research (AIR) in Palo Alto, California. She received the Ph.D. in social psychology in 1971 from Carnegie-Mellon University and became assistant professor of psychology at the Ateneo University in the Philippines. In 1972 she returned to the United States, and from 1972 to 1973, she was a research psychologist at the Suicide Prevention Research Project, Information and Volunteer Services, Pittsburgh. Since joining the staff of AIR in 1973, she has directed a number of social-science research studies in the areas of population (fertility, teenage pregnancy, migration) and career development. Results of these studies have been published in numerous AIR technical reports and in scholarly journals such as *Demography, Social Biology, Family Planning Perspectives, Journal of Population, Journal of Vocational Behavior, Medical Aspects of Human Sexuality, Philippine Journal of Psychology, Sex Roles, and Philippine Sociological Review.*